Rigby
PM Math Readers

Teacher's Guide

Emergent
Stages A and B

Rigby PM Math Readers Teacher's Guide, Emergent, Stages A and B

Published by Rigby
a division of Harcourt Supplemental Publishers, Inc.
1000 Hart Road
Barrington, IL 60010-2627
www.rigby.com

Copyright © 2004 Rigby
a division of Harcourt Supplemental Publishers, Inc.

Text © Jenny Giles, Elsie Nelley and Annette Smith 2002
Illustrations © Nelson Australia Pty Ltd 2002

Cover and text photographs by Lindsay Edwards and Bill Thomas
Edited by Angelique Campbell-Muir
Designed by Sonia Juraja
Illustrated by Boris Silvestri

All rights reserved. No part of this publication may be reproduced or transmitted in any form or by any means, electronic or mechanical, including photocopying, recording, taping, or any information storage and retrieval system, without permission in writing from the Publisher. Contact: Rigby Copyright Permissions, PO Box 26015, Austin, Texas 78759.

Rigby® is a trademark of Reed Elsevier Inc. registered in the United States and/or other jurisdictions.

First published in 2002 by Nelson Thomson Learning

10 9 8 7 6 5 4 3 2 1
08 07 06 05 04 03

Printed in the United States of America

ISBN 0 7578-7414-2

Contents

Introduction
The PM Philosophy	4
Rigby PM Math Readers and the PM Philosophy	6
Rigby PM Math Readers in the Classroom	8
Rigby PM Math Readers Curriculum Overview	10
Using the Rigby PM Math Readers Teacher's Guides	

Teacher's Notes Stage A
One Picture	16
A Picnic for Two	20
We Can See Three	24
Four Cars	28
Five Birds and Five Mice	32
Red Block, Blue Block	36
Counting Down	40
Big Shapes and Little Shapes	44
A Game with Shapes	48
Making a Butterfly	52
Long and Short	56
Sorting Leaves	60

Teacher's Notes Stage B
Days of the Week	64
As Heavy As	68
Shapes with a Rope	72
Making Party Hats	76
Boxes, Cans, and Balls	80
Six Under the Sea	84
Seven in a Line	88
From One to Eight	92
Nine Children at the Pool	96
Five and Five Are Ten	100
Ten Frogs for the Pond	104
Animal Graphs	108

PM Math Concepts and PM Reading Levels   112

The PM Philosophy

The philosophy that supports all the material in the Rigby PMs is based on the teaching, writings, and research of Dame Marie Clay, Warwick Elley (NZCER), and the pioneering work at the Department of Education, New Zealand.

Simply expressed the PM philosophy is this:

- children learn to read well if they are encouraged to use a variety of skills, processes, and behaviors, rather than a particular method
- when children are learning to read, they should be given materials that have been carefully crafted to meet their needs; books that give them *success, enjoyment,* and *understanding*

This is so that children are not confused by being asked to process too many unknown words on a page. Each book has been leveled to avoid "frustration level" reading. All PM titles have been written using carefully selected vocabulary.

In each successive book in the series, beyond level 5, there is a very low ratio of new word introduction (at most 1:20).

The text, illustrations, and page layouts of all books in the PM series have been designed so that children can:

- develop the right concepts about print
- acquire a growing number of high frequency words
- build and use a storehouse of known words
- use visual, syntactical, and semantic cues to derive meaning from text
- apply reasoning and prediction skills
- link the reading and writing processes
- practice self-extending skills

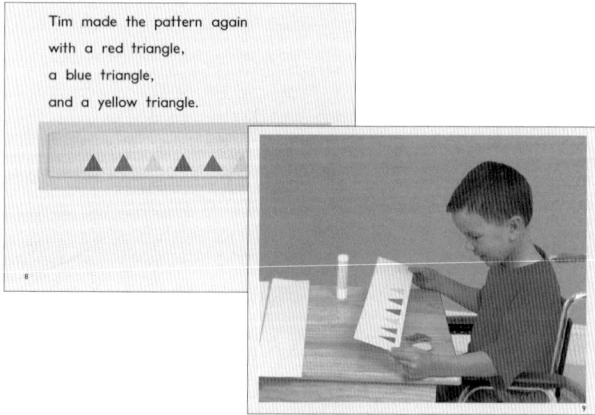

Success

The PM materials allow children continual opportunities for developing the skills, processes, and behaviors needed to become successful readers. Each title is completely child-centered and full of meaning. *Meaning is paramount in the Rigby PMs.*

Because success matters, a very *gentle learning gradient* or *leveling system* has been created.

Illustrations and photographs should help children interpret the story, and add to their success and understanding. Attention is paid to the *close match of text and illustration* in a PM book. The illustration style is most often realistic, thereby enhancing and giving depth to the child's understanding of the story.

Adequate space between letters, words, and lines is provided so that each letter and word can be seen clearly. Each line break and page break is carefully considered so that it contributes to the meaning of the story.

Enjoyment

When children read a Rigby PM book they know they will taste success and that contributes to their enjoyment. Without success enjoyment of reading is impossible.

Enjoyment is one of the intrinsic rewards of reading. Good readers do a great deal of reading for enjoyment. Reading involves attending to several things at once and it is only with pleasurable reading texts that such behaviors fall into place.

Sustained enjoyment comes from the child-centered high-interest topics, the beautiful illustrations, and the vital ingredient – a storyline. Proper story structure puts life into the simplest books by capturing and holding the reader's attention. No matter how long or how short the story, or how many variations appear to be woven in it, each Rigby PM story follows the same traditional pattern: the central character(s) has a problem, and by the end of the book the problem is solved in a satisfactory way. The logic of the story helps children to understand.

The aim of the Rigby PMs is to make children feel good about themselves by enhancing their self-esteem. Enjoyment comes from the acceptance of the variety of lifestyles, types of families, and ethnic groups. Rigby PM books allow every child to find a character with whom they can identify. The portrayals of various types of communities reflects the real world to which children belong, and so adds to everyone's understanding and enjoyment.

Understanding

The concepts in the first reading books must be understood by the very young if they are to become successful readers. Without understanding there can be no self-correction. Understanding is increased by carefully drawn illustrations and well-selected photographs that illuminate the text and deepen the meaning. Insights come from viewing as well as reading.

Understanding comes from scientific accuracy too. Nonfiction should be as accurate as the author can possibly make it, but fiction too, should respect accuracy. The authors supply much reference and research material to the illustrators so that all books are as accurate as possible in terms of scientific detail, landscape, and historical background.

Meaning shapes every page, every paragraph, every sentence, every phrase, and every choice of word. Meaning is embedded in every Rigby PM book, both fiction and nonfiction.

There are over 700 fiction and nonfiction books in the Rigby PM program. They cover fantasy, history, natural history, technology, verse, songs, and plays. Children approach reading from many different angles. A wide variety of subjects and genres provides a range of choices. This helps teachers make the right match between book and child.

Success, enjoyment, and understanding make the task of learning to read worthwhile, and help turn young children into self-motivating, self-correcting, self-extending achievers. With the right teaching, the Rigby PM books will open up children's minds, challenge their thinking, and stir their understanding.

Rigby PM Math Readers and the PM Philosophy

Rigby PM Math Readers support successful learning in mathematics during the early years:

- All texts follow the PM tradition of a meaningful context.
- Mathematical concepts are developed through a literacy approach that links reading and mathematical stages of development.
- A gradual reading Level System supports the learner.
- Both high-frequency vocabulary and mathematical vocabulary have been carefully selected and are introduced gradually.
- There is a careful match between text and illustrations or photographs.

Rigby PM Math Readers enhance understanding and application of mathematical concepts and strategies:

- Concepts are developed sequentially.
- Children are able to read the texts and concentrate on the mathematical concepts.

- New ideas link to prior knowledge and understandings.
- Texts include essential mathematical vocabulary relevant to early stages of development.
- The texts recognize that children learn in different ways at different rates of progress.

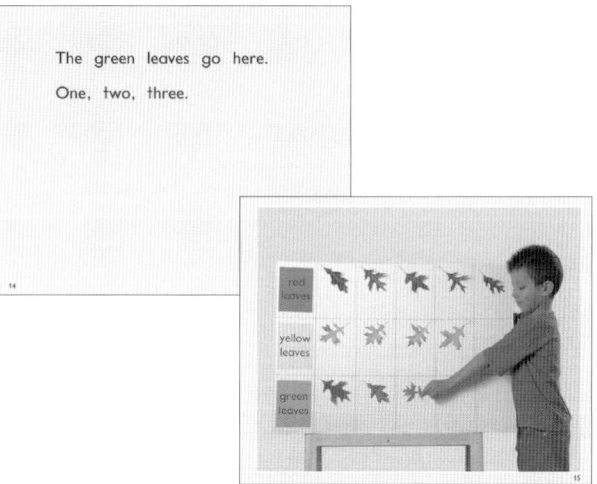

Rigby PM Math Readers present mathematical concepts in contexts that are meaningful and relevant to the learner:

- Contexts match and extend children's spoken and thinking vocabulary.
- Contexts reflect the real world to which children belong and include a variety of life styles, families, and ethnic groups.
- Equipment and materials are relevant to the learning.
- Emphasis is on using real objects in meaningful situations.
- Equipment used is available in most schools.
- Activities can be adapted to meet the needs of particular groups of children.

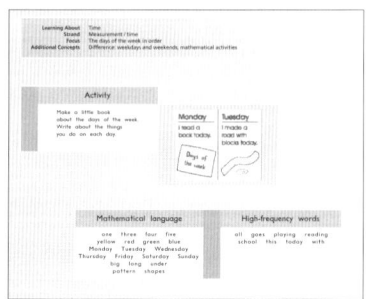

Rigby PM Math Readers challenge children's thinking:

- Problems are presented in realistic contexts.
- Question and answer opportunities reinforce and extend mathematical discovery.
- Accurate photographs and illustrations stimulate discussion.
- The Teacher's Guides include additional activities.
- Contexts encourage predicting, checking, and confirming of ideas being explored.
- Problem solving is central to all texts.

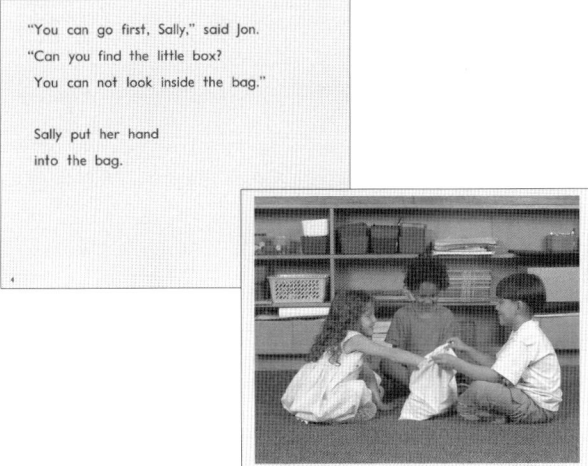

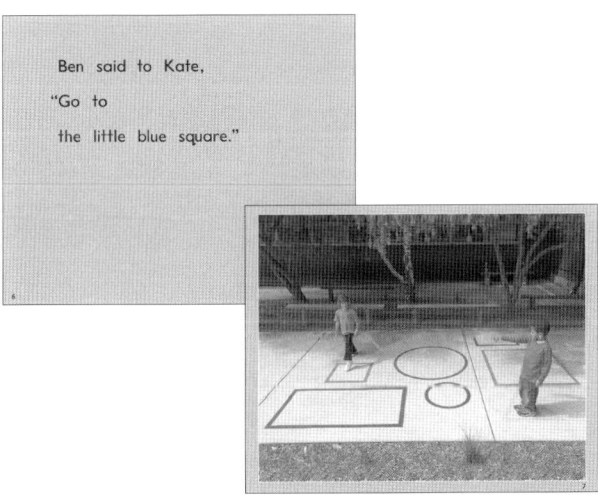

Rigby PM Math Readers encourage confidence and independence:

- Children can read the books independently.
- Children are gradually introduced to the writing of math concepts through meaningful situations and examples.
- Children can utilize the texts and pictures to practice the activities.
- Discussion encourages communication of ideas.
- Blackline masters provide follow-up activities that are linked to concept development.

Rigby PM Math Readers foster enjoyment:

- Success motivates enjoyment and enthusiasm.
- Children feel good about themselves when they apply knowledge and strategies with understanding.
- Each stage contains a "Making" book.
- Early blackline masters include poems that are fun and enhance understanding.
- Some books include humorous situations.
- Books can be shared and enjoyed at home.
- Many characters appear in more than one book.
- The books offer opportunities for children to interact, communicate, and co-operate with others.

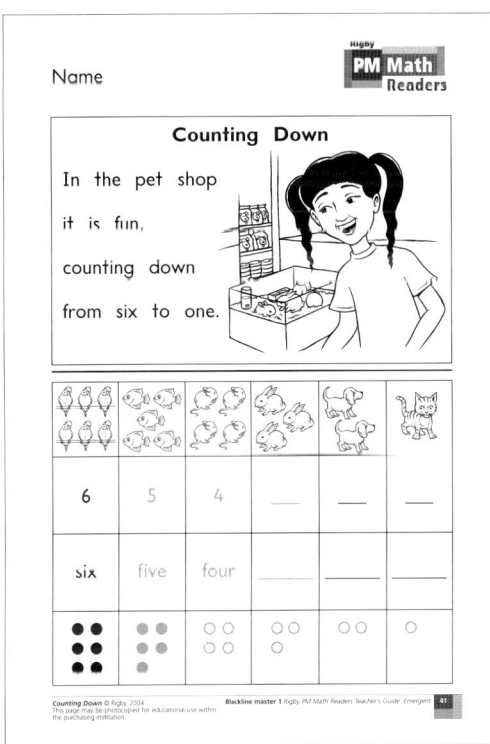

Rigby PM Math Readers Teacher's Guide: Emergent

Rigby PM Math Readers in the Classroom

Rigby PM Math Readers have been designed to support a range of classroom mathematics programs, and are closely linked with curriculum topics at each level. Many of the books outline procedures which utilize the standard mathematical equipment found in most schools, while others feature familiar everyday materials. This means that the procedures outlined in the books can be reinforced and extended in a variety of practical classroom situations, and children can be involved in problem-solving activities.

The program consists of four levels, or stages:

Stages A and B are appropriate for Kindergarten and First Grade classrooms.

Stages C and D are appropriate for First Grade classrooms.

Throughout all the stages, each book features basic mathematical concepts and procedures that are outlined in simple terms, using high-frequency vocabulary that is appropriate for the level. It is the same high-frequency vocabulary that has been used in the *Rigby PM Collection* and *PM Plus* programs, so that children who can read at Levels 1–3, for example, will be able to read the corresponding *Rigby PM Math Readers* at Stage A.

Rigby PM Math Readers feature:

- relevant mathematical terminology, introduced and integrated with the high-frequency vocabulary at an appropriate rate and reinforced in successive books

- texts that are supported by clear photographs or illustrations, together with numerals, that have been produced in a format which is easily recognized by young children

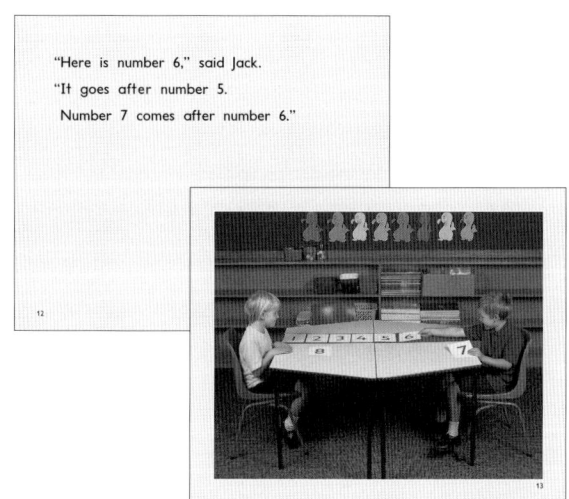

Rigby PM Math Readers Teacher's Guide: Emergent

- topics which are presented in familiar child-centered situations that enable young children to read and understand basic mathematical concepts

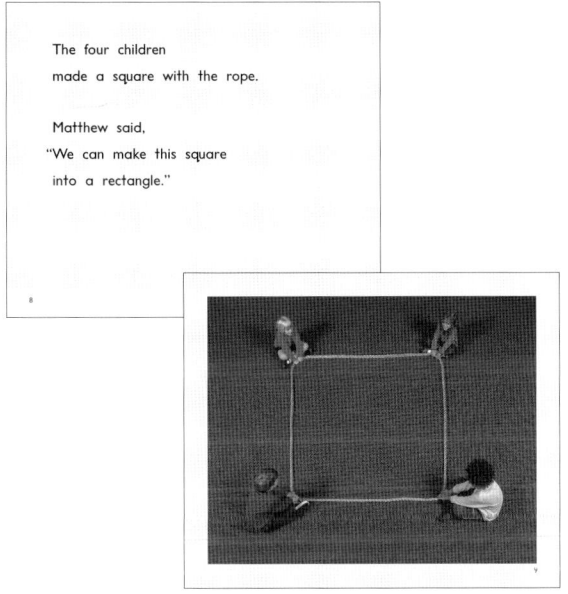

- one main concept in each book with two or more additional concepts being integrated
- established methods of investigating and recording mathematical data

Rigby PM Math Readers are suitable for use in a variety of teaching and learning situations including:

- shared class lessons
- group and individual instruction
- independent or paired reading
- follow-up activities
- introductions and conclusions to lessons

For the English Language Learner

The books are a valuable resource for children whose second language is English, and also for those children who may have verbal and practical computational skills, but less advanced reading skills. Children who have difficulty understanding written procedures and directions are often unable to do what is required of them, although they may possess the necessary mathematical knowledge. *Rigby PM Math Readers* develop and reinforce reading and mathematical skills together in carefully leveled stages.

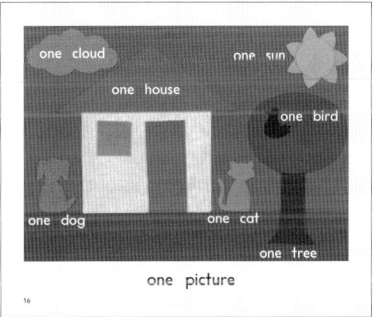

For Home Interaction

The books are particularly suitable for home interaction – parents and caregivers will be able to relate to the familiar mathematical procedures that are featured in everyday situations throughout the levels, and their understanding of curriculum content can be enhanced through home use.

The comprehensive Teacher's Guides offer support in the form of an instructional page for each book together with three blackline master pages. A verse directly related to the text is a feature of the first blackline master. These verses can be included in class or individual anthologies, or enlarged as poem cards. The blackline masters can also be utilized for practical assessment purposes.

Curriculum Overview

Stage A
Magenta-Red – Kindergarten/First Grade

Title	Topic	Strand	Focus	Additional Concepts
One Picture	Learning about one	Number	Linking numeral/word/object	Positioning, sequencing
A Picnic for Two	Learning about two	Number	One-to-one correspondence	Counting, grouping
We Can See Three	Learning about three	Number	Classifying/grouping	Counting, positioning
Four Cars	Learning about four	Number	Counting groups to four	Addition, positional vocabulary
Five Birds and Five Mice	Learning about five	Number	Counting groups to five	Prediction, positional vocabulary
Red Block, Blue Block	Learning about two-element patterns	Number	Two-element repeating pattern	Counting, positioning
Counting Down	Learning about groups	Number	Groups in descending order	Sequencing, grouping
Big Shapes and Little Shapes	Learning about shapes	Shape and space	Recognizing two-dimensional shapes	Color, comparison
A Game with Shapes	Learning about position, direction, and movement	Shape and space	Following instructions	Shape, color, size
Making a Butterfly	Learning about symmetry	Shape and space	Making a symmetrical design	Sequencing, color
Long and Short	Learning about length	Measurement	Comparison of long and short	Movement, positional vocabulary
Sorting Leaves	Learning about classification	Data	Classifying by color	Sorting, grouping

Rigby PM Math Readers Teacher's Guide: Emergent

Curriculum Overview

Stage B
Yellow-Blue – Kindergarten/First Grade

Title	Topic	Strand	Focus	Additional Concepts
Days of the Week	Learning about time	Measurement/time	The days of the week in order	Difference: weekdays and weekends, mathematical activities
Ten Frogs for the Pond	Learning about chance	Number	Probability and chance	Addition, the empty set, zero
As Heavy As	Learning about mass	Measurement	Comparing weight and size	Estimation, confirmation
Making Party Hats	Learning about three-element patterns	Number	Patterning with three repeating elements	Two-dimensional shapes, sequencing
Boxes, Cans, and Balls	Learning about three-dimensional shapes	Shape and space	Identifying three-dimensional shapes by touch	Properties of three-dimensional shapes, probability
Six Under the Sea	Learning about six	Number	Groups of six in a range of patterns	Cardinal names and numbers, position and movement
Seven in a Line	Learning about seven	Number	Sequencing seven objects according to size	Three-dimensional shapes, ordinal names
From One to Eight	Learning about eight	Number	Numerical order	Position and direction, ordinal names
Nine Children at the Pool	Learning about nine	Number	Compensation of a number	Addends of nine, ordered and disordered groups
Five and Five are Ten	Learning about ten	Number	Conservation of a number	Counting, addition
Shapes with a Rope	Learning about the formation of shapes	Shape and space	Properties of two-dimensional shapes	Prediction, following directions
Anima Graphs	Learning about graphs	Data	Grouping and comparing	Analyzing data, part/whole relationships

Rigby PM Math Readers Teacher's Guide: Emergent

Curriculum Overview

Stage C*
Blue-Green – First Grade

Title	Topic	Strand	Focus	Additional Concepts
One More Frog	Exploring addition	Number	Add one: introduction of plus equation	Addends, comparing
Win a Prize!	Exploring subtraction	Number	Take away one: introduction of minus equation	Counting, comparing
The Take-away Puppy	Exploring addition and subtraction	Number	Addition and subtraction as complementary processes	Ordinal numbers, counting, and comparing
Take Two	Exploring sets	Number	Comparing sets less than ten and more than ten	Counting backward by two, minus equations
Grouping Shells	Exploring sets	Number	Comparing sets less than ten and more than ten	Recording, estimating, and confirming
Twenty Steps to the Treasure	Exploring addition to twenty	Number	Using the number line as a tool for addition	Ordinal numbers, reading and interpreting mathematical instructions
Eleven on a Team	Exploring joining of groups	Number	Addition: sum becomes first addend of next equation	Counting on, recording plus equations
A Game of Bowling	Exploring addition to twenty	Number	Addition: three addends	Counting on, recording scores
Two Halves and Two Quarters	Exploring fractions	Number	Introduction of fractions: a half and a quarter	Part whole relationships, fractions of two and three-dimensional objects
Making a Castle	Exploring three-dimensional construction	Shape and Space	Forming and utilizing three-dimensional shapes	Properties of three-dimensional shapes, following a procedure
Animal Symmetry	Exploring symmetry	Shape and Space	Symmetrical patterns in nature	Comparison, design
Favorite Books	Exploring data	Data	Collecting and classifying data	Assembling data, interpreting data

* See Rigby PM Math Readers Teacher's Guide: Early

Rigby PM Math Readers Teacher's Guide: Emergent

Curriculum Overview

Stage D*
Orange-Turquoise – First Grade

Title	Topic	Strand	Focus	Additional Concepts
Lucy's Garden	Exploring odd and even sets	Number	Doubles and near-doubles to ten in sequence	Odd and even sets, comparing sets
Billy's Sticker Book	Exploring multiplication strategies	Number	Working with two equal sets	Doubles to twelve, equivalent groups
Sets of Picture Cards	Exploring addition and subtraction	Number	Comparing sets and working with symbols	Comparing sets, describing relationships
Fourteen Marbles	Exploring place value	Number	Grouping and recording addends of a two-digit number	Place value, recording equations
Apples for Sale	Exploring numbers from a base of ten	Number	Addition of units between ten and twenty	Counting on from a base of ten, the teen numbers
Snail Trail to 100	Exploring the 100 board	Number	Working with two-digit numbers	Place value, movement, and position
The Junior Concert	Exploring multiples of ten	Number	Addition in tens to 100	Grouping in tens, multiplication
Billy, the Number Champ	Exploring number relationships	Number	Understanding basic facts	Counting on, addition facts to ten
The Secret Message	Exploring a number code	Number	Using decoding strategies	Problem solving, the passage of time
Twelve Balloons for the Clown	Exploring problem-solving procedures	Number	Following a set procedure	Half of a quantity, comparison of sets with a sum of twelve
Making a Clock Cake	Exploring time	Measurement	Time on a clock face: hour, half-hour, quarter hour	Numbers associated with telling the time, fractions
The Class Photograph	Exploring height	Measurement	Sequential order of height	Estimation and comparison, ordinal numbers to twenty

* See Rigby PM Math Readers Teacher's Guide: Early

Using the Rigby PM Math Readers

There are four pages of notes in the Teacher's Guides for every *Rigby PM Math Readers* title. The first page consists of notes on teaching procedures; the other three pages consist of blackline masters that are directly related to the text focus.

Headings
These indicate:
a) the theme of the text
b) the curriculum strand
c) the main concept focus
d) the other concepts included in the text

About the book
A brief description of the theme of the book, the mathematical focus, and the characters involved.

Numerals
A list of numerals contained in the book.

Links with other PM Books
Books from the *PM Collection*, *PM Plus*, and *Rigby PM Math Readers* series, which have a similar theme or focus.

High-Frequency Words
These words are selected from the appropriate PM reading level and are introduced slowly.

Mathematical Language
Vocabulary that is math-related, including number names, names of shapes, and positional and procedural vocabulary. This math language is introduced as interest words, which are reinforced throughout the series.

Reinforcing the Concept
Further guidance is provided, sometimes in the form of relevant math games, to help reinforce understanding of the main concept.

Focusing on the Concept
The cover pictures and title page vignettes have been designed to highlight the theme of the text. Detailed page notes show how the concept can be explained and clarified.

Discovering Additional Concepts
At least two additional concepts have been included in each text. These are listed together with suggestions for extending the children's knowledge of topics and procedures.

Using the blackline masters
Precise instructions are given for best use of each of the three blackline masters.

Stage A Book 1
One Picture

Learning About Strand	One Number
Focus	Linking numeral/word/object
Additional Concepts	Positioning, sequencing

Links with other Rigby PM Books
Up in the sky (PM Plus Starters 1)
Look at the house (PM Plus Starters 1)
In the garden (PM Plus Starters 1)

About the Book
A child forms an environmental picture using felt templates as a medium. A variety of objects, one of each kind, are placed on a plain background.

Mathematical language	High-frequency words	Numeral
one	look, at, the	1

Focusing on the concept

- *Cover and title page:* Discuss the picture and the way in which it features only one of each item. Connect the word **one** with the numeral **1** and the pattern of one on the title-page icon.
  Extra focus: The number 1 comes first in the sequence of numbers.
- *Pages 2–3:* Read aloud the text and relate it to the picture. Comment on the fact that the house has one door and one window.
- *Pages 4–15:* Reinforce the concept of **one** on these pages, making connections between the text, pictures, and captions.
- *Page 16:* Study and discuss the labels. Ask the children to name the only object in the picture of which there can never be more than one.

Reinforcing the concept

- Using the Rigby PM Plus books listed above, focus on the single item shown on each of the pages. Connect with the number 1. Make captions for these pages, such as *one plane*.
- Make a chart of mathematical items and label them, such as *1 ruler, 1 square*.

Discovering additional concepts

- **Positioning:** Discuss the reasons for placing the items in their positions in the picture. Look at other acceptable positions for the items.
- **Sequencing:** Explain how the same picture could have been formed if the items had been put on in reverse order.

Using the blackline masters

1. Read the text and color the pictures. Trace and complete the numerals, words, and pattern.
2. Cut out the labels and place them by items found in the classroom. Color the pictures to match the items in the classroom.
3. Trace over the gray words and color the pictures to match those in the book.

Using the Blackline Masters

Three blackline masters have been provided for each title in *Rigby PM Math Readers*, including brief instructions. It is suggested that teachers discuss the instructions thoroughly before asking the children to complete the exercises independently.

The book can be used to support the exercises, and in many cases, classroom materials can be used to clarify the procedures. Further exercises, or a related illustration, can be completed on the backside of the page. Many of the blackline masters are suitable for assessment purposes.

The first blackline master has been designed for use as two separate exercises for younger children. The top half consists of a short verse based on vocabulary from the text, and is supported by a picture. This verse can be used in individual or class anthologies, or enlarged as a poem card for shared reading. The vocabulary in the verse is appropriate for the reading level of the book.

The lower half consists of written practice exercises based on the book topic, such as the writing of a numeral and its related word, pattern, and picture.

The second blackline master is based directly on the main concept contained in the book.

The third blackline master provides an extension exercise.

Rigby PM Math Readers Teacher's Guide: Emergent   15

Stage A Book 1
One Picture

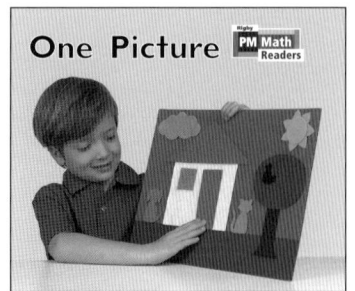

Learning About	One
Strand	Number
Focus	Linking numeral/word/object
Additional Concepts	Positioning, sequencing

Links with other Rigby PM Books
Up in the sky (PM Plus Starters 1)
Look at the house (PM Plus Starters 1)
In the garden (PM Plus Starters 1)

About the Book
A child forms an environmental picture using felt templates as a medium. A variety of objects, one of each kind, are placed on a plain background.

Mathematical language	High-frequency words	Numeral
one	look, at, the	1

Focusing on the concept

- *Cover and title page:* Discuss the picture and the way in which it features only one of each item. Connect the word **one** with the numeral **1** and the pattern of one on the title-page icon.
  <u>Extra focus:</u> The number 1 comes first in the sequence of numbers.
- *Pages 2–3:* Read aloud the text and relate it to the picture. Comment on the fact that the house has one door and one window.
- *Pages 4–15:* Reinforce the concept of **one** on these pages, making connections between the text, pictures, and captions.
- *Page 16:* Study and discuss the labels. Ask the children to name the only object in the picture of which there can never be more than one.

Reinforcing the concept

- Using the Rigby PM Plus books listed above, focus on the single item shown on each of the pages. Connect with the number 1. Make captions for these pages, such as *one plane*.
- Make a chart of mathematical items and label them, such as *1 ruler, 1 square*.

Discovering additional concepts

- **Positioning:** Discuss the reasons for placing the items in their positions in the picture. Look at other acceptable positions for the items.
- **Sequencing:** Explain how the same picture could have been formed if the items had been put on in reverse order.

Using the blackline masters

1. Read the text and color the pictures. Trace and complete the numerals, words, and pattern.
2. Cut out the labels and place them by items found in the classroom. Color the pictures to match the items in the classroom.
3. Trace over the gray words and color the pictures to match those in the book.

Name _____

One Picture

Here is a picture.

It's all about one.

One house, one tree,

one cloud, one sun.

1	1	1	___	___
one	one	one	___	___
●	●	○	○	

One Picture © Rigby, 2004.
This page may be photocopied for educational use within the purchasing institution.

Blackline master 1 *Rigby PM Math Readers Teacher's Guide: Emergent*

Name _____

One book

One pencil

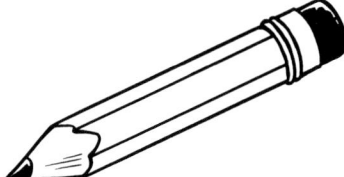

One circle

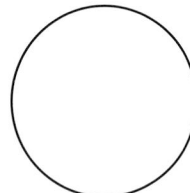

One square

One triangle

One rectangle

Name _____

Look at the **tree.**

One **tree.**

Look at the **sun.**

One **sun.**

Look at the **cat.**

One **cat.**

Look at the **dog.**

One **dog.**

One Picture © Rigby, 2004.
This page may be photocopied for educational use within the purchasing institution.

Blackline master 3 *Rigby PM Math Readers Teacher's Guide: Emergent*

Stage A Book 2
A Picnic for Two

Learning About	Two
Strand	Number
Focus	One-to-one correspondence
Additional Concepts	Counting, grouping

Links with other PM Books
Two eyes, two ears (PM Nonfiction Levels 5/6)
Eggs for breakfast (PM Nonfiction Levels 5/6)
Two little ducks get lost (PM Plus Level 10)

About the Book
Two children take turns to share food equally at a picnic in their backyard. The groups of two items become one for each child.

Mathematical language	High-frequency words	Numeral
one, two, little	and, can, for, I, is, me, see, we, you	2

Focusing on the concept

- *Cover and title page:* Study the sharing procedure as it relates to one-to-one correspondence. Connect this procedure with the numbers **two** and **one**. Discuss the contents of the lunch box and connect with the icon.
- *Pages 2–7:* Predict what the children are going to do next and reinforce the sharing procedure. (Each sandwich has been cut from a whole into two halves.) Note that the drink bottles (not mentioned in the text) have already been allocated.
- *Pages 8–16:* Continue to make text–picture connections. Introduce the word **empty** when discussing the lunch box on pages 13 and 15.

Reinforcing the concept

- Read the book *Two eyes, two ears* to the children. Extend the concept to two arms, two legs, etc. Relate to the term "a pair", such as a pair of socks, a pair of shoes, etc.
- Use classroom items to focus on one-to-one correspondence. Children can distribute books, pencils, etc.

Discovering additional concepts

- **Counting:** Encourage children to count the books and pencils and correlate these equal groups before distributing (see procedure above).
- **Grouping:** Develop this procedure further during recess-like activities, such as forming equal teams.

Using the blackline masters

1. Read the text and color the pictures. Trace and complete the numerals, words, and pattern.
2. Trace over the gray words and numerals. Complete and color the pictures.
3. Trace over the gray words. Add words to spaces. Color the pictures to match those in the book.

Name _____

A Picnic for Two

Here are the apples and sandwiches.

Here are the little cakes, too.

We are having a picnic…

a picnic for me and for you.

👧👦	🍎🍎	🥪🥪	🧁🧁	🧴🧴
2	2	2	___	___
two	two	two		
●●	●●	○○	○○	

A Picnic for Two © Rigby, 2004.
This page may be photocopied for educational use within the purchasing institution.

Blackline master 1 *Rigby PM Math Readers Teacher's Guide: Emergent* 21

Name _____

I can see two **apples.**

2 **apples**

I can see two **sandwiches.**

2 **sandwiches**

I can see two **cakes.**

2 **cakes**

I can see two **bananas.**

2 **bananas**

A Picnic for Two © Rigby, 2004.
This page may be photocopied for educational use within the purchasing institution.

Blackline master 2 *Rigby PM Math Readers Teacher's Guide: Emergent*

Name _____

Here are two apples.

One apple is for you.

_____ apple is for me.

Here are two sandwiches.

_____ sandwich is for you.

_____ sandwich is for me.

Here are two cakes.

_____ cake is for you.

_____ cake is for me.

A Picnic for Two © Rigby, 2004.
This page may be photocopied for educational use within the purchasing institution.

Blackline master 3 *Rigby PM Math Readers Teacher's Guide: Emergent* 23

Stage A Book 3

We Can See Three

Learning About	Three
Strand	Number
Focus	Classifying/grouping
Additional Concepts	Counting, positioning

Links with other PM Books
Sam and Bingo (PM Plus Level 3)
Mother Tiger & her cubs (PM Plus Level 11)
Clever Brown Mouse (PM Plus Level 13)

About the Book
Three children make a toy farm consisting of three enclosures. They each select a group of three animals of the same species and place these groups in separate enclosures.

Mathematical language	High-frequency words	Numeral
one, two, three, little	a, and, are, at, can, for, go, here, is, look, the	3

Focusing on the concept

- *Cover and title page:* Discuss the reasons why the animals are in groups and in three enclosures. Make connections between the three children and the three groups of three animals. Connect also with the icon.
- *Pages 2–3:* Examine the disordered group of animals in the photo and compare with the ordered groups on the cover. Ask the children to predict what the procedure might be.
- *Pages 4–15:* Make text, picture, and caption connections.
- *Page 16:* Emphasize the number three, for example three enclosures with three animals in each; three groups of animals.

Reinforcing the concept

- Discuss similarities within the groups, such as four legs, two eyes, two ears, and one tail.
- Examine criteria other than species for classifying and grouping, such as size, color, shape, and pattern.

Discovering additional concepts

- **Counting:** Count the number of animals on page 3 and page 15. Discuss the advantages of counting ordered groups of items in comparison with disordered groups.
- **Positioning:** Discuss placing the animals in groups with a common attribute as an effective way of classifying. Extend this concept using classroom materials.

Using the blackline masters

1. Read the verse and color the pictures. Trace and complete the numerals, words, and pattern.
2. Trace over the gray words and numerals. Color the pictures.
3. Trace over the gray words. Cut out the animals and place each in its correct enclosure on the farm.

Name _____

We Can See Three

Down on the farm,

we can see

cows, sheep, and horses...

one, two, three.

3	3	3	___	___
three	three	three	_____	_____

We Can See Three © Rigby, 2004.
This page may be photocopied for educational use within the purchasing institution.

Blackline master 1 *Rigby PM Math Readers Teacher's Guide: Emergent* 25

Name _____

I can see three horses.

One, two, three horses

1, 2, 3 horses

3 horses.

I can see three cows.

One, two, three cows

1, 2, 3 cows

3 cows.

I can see three sheep.

One, two, three sheep

1, 2, 3 sheep

3 sheep.

Name _____

Here is a farm.

Three horses, three cows,

and three sheep are on the farm.

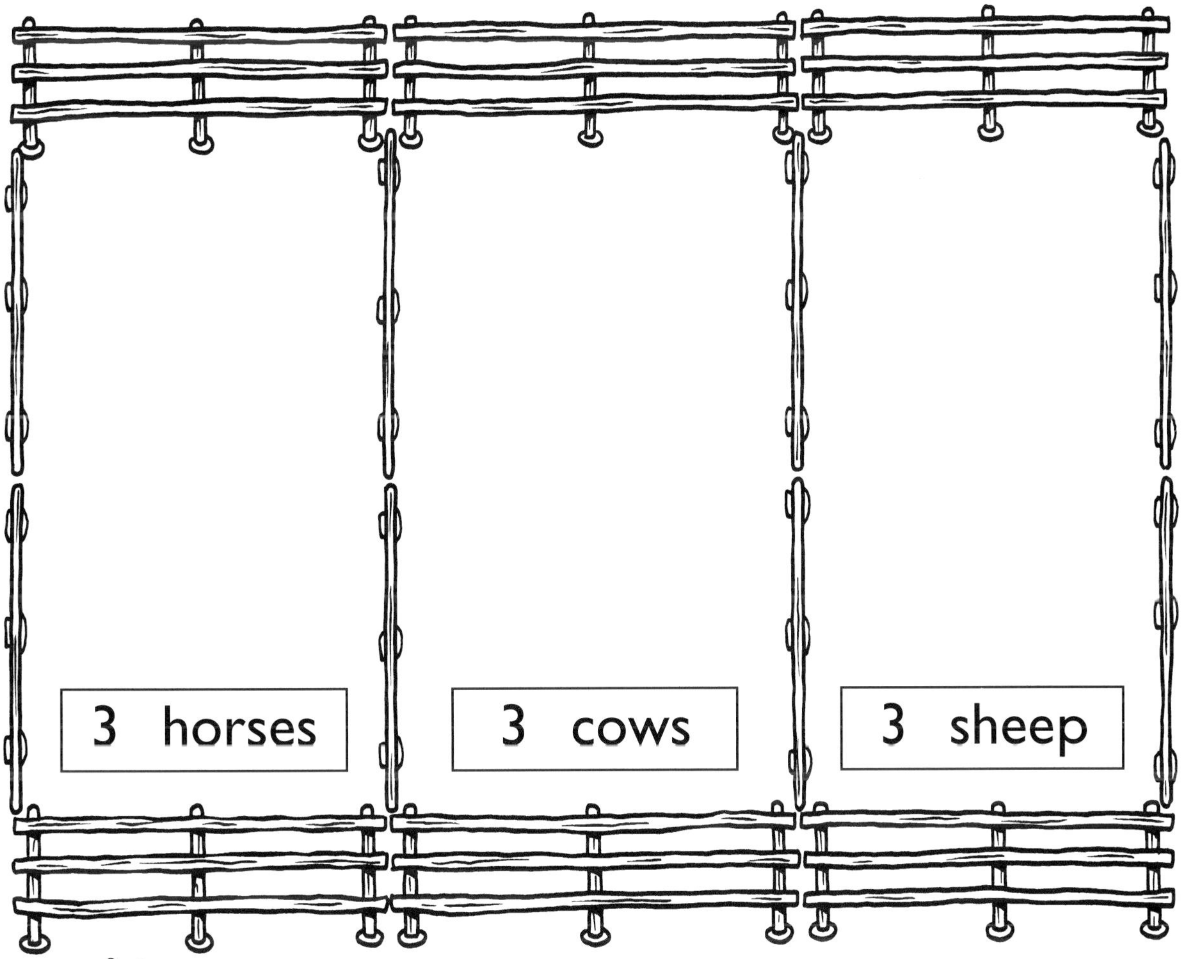

| 3 horses | 3 cows | 3 sheep |

We Can See Three © Rigby, 2004.
This page may be photocopied for educational use within the purchasing institution.

Blackline master 3 *Rigby PM Math Readers Teacher's Guide: Emergent* 27

Stage A Book 4
Four Cars

Learning About	Four
Strand	Number
Focus	Counting groups to four
Additional Concepts	Addition, positional vocabulary

Links with other PM Books
Four ice creams (PM Plus Starters 2)
Billy can count (PM Plus Level 6)
Sam's race (PM Plus Level 4)

About the Book
Two children, using four toy cars, form groups to a sum of four using the addends 3 and 1, 2 and 2, and 1 and 3. As the cars are moved into a garage, the different groupings are started in the text.

Mathematical language	High-frequency words	Numerals
one, two, three, four, in	and, are, going, here, in, is, not, the, to	1, 2, 3, 4

Focusing on the concept

- *Cover and title page:* Make connections with the number of cars and the word **Four** in the title. Count the cars, then discuss the two groups of two as the cars are shared between the children.
- *Title page:* Help the children to recognize the connections between the picture of the cars and the numeral/word/pattern for four.
- *Pages 2–15:* Discuss the progression of the cars from their position outside the garage to their position inside the garage. Make connections between the text and the picture on each page, noting that the single-file line outside the garage changes to a horizontal line inside the garage.
- *Page 16:* Make connections between the numerals and the pictures, noting that the cars are now facing the reader.

Reinforcing the concept

- Using classroom materials, encourage the children to make groups of four objects within a given space. Move the position of these items into the groupings shown in the book. Check by counting that the total number of items remains constant throughout.

Discovering additional concepts

- **Addition:** Discuss the use of the word **and** when it connects numerals, as the simplest form of numerical addition.
- **Positional vocabulary:** Emphasize the phrases "in the garage" and "not in the garage." Introduce other positional vocabulary orally, such as **out, next to, behind, in front of, following,** and **beside.**

Using the blackline masters

1. Read the verse and color the pictures. Trace and complete the numerals, words, and pattern.
2. Trace over the gray words and numerals. Complete the words and numerals in the final statement. Color the cars.
3. Trace over the gray numerals and color the gray number patterns. Add number patterns to the spaces.

Name _____

Four Cars

Cars in the garage,

one, two, three.

The last little car

is here by me.

4	4	4	___	___
four	four	four	_____	_____
●● ●●	●● ●●	○○ ○○	○○ ○○	

Four Cars © Rigby, 2004.
This page may be photocopied for educational use within the purchasing institution.

Blackline master 1 *Rigby PM Math Readers Teacher's Guide: Emergent* 29

Rigby PM Math Readers

Name ______________________

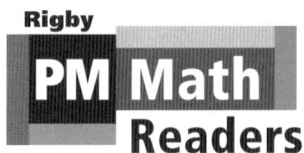

Here are four cars.

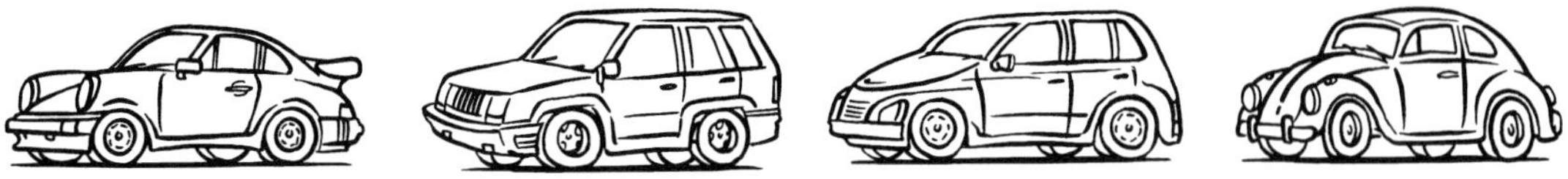

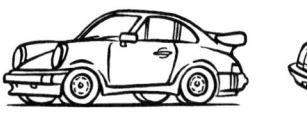

1 2 3 4

One car and three cars

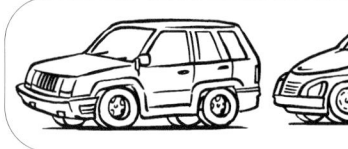

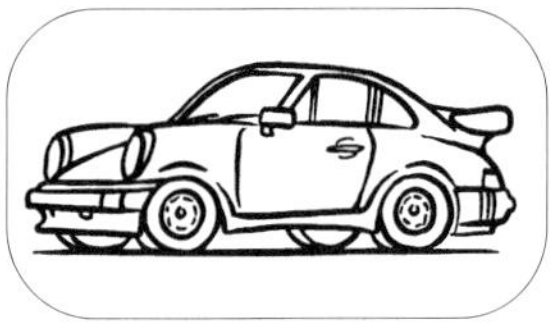

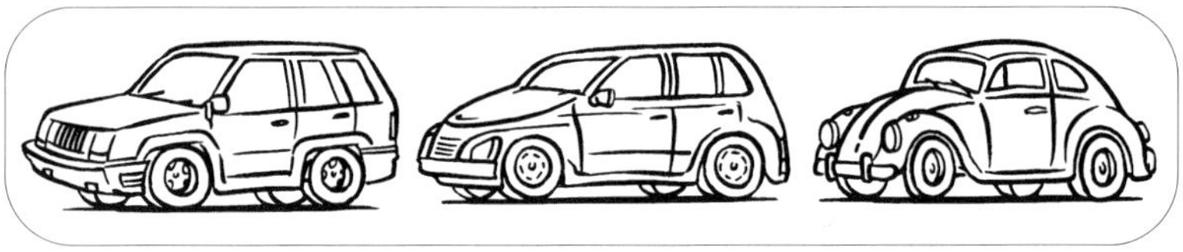

1 2 3 4

Two cars and two cars

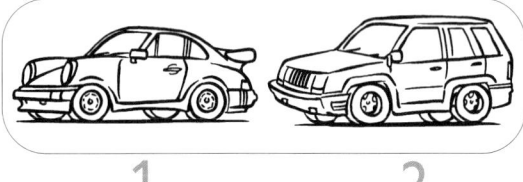

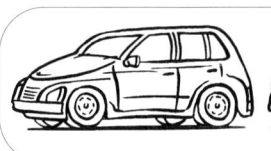

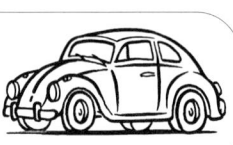

1 2 3 4

________ cars and ________ car

_____ _____ _____ _____

Name _____

1   and   3   make   4

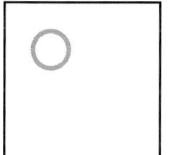 +  =

2   and   2   make   4

 + 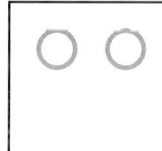 =

3   and   1   make   4

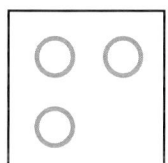 + 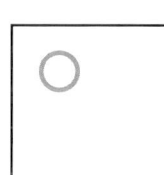 =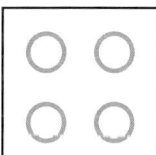

4   and   0   make   4

 +  =

Four Cars © Rigby, 2004.
This page may be photocopied for educational use within the purchasing institution.

Blackline master 3 *Rigby PM Math Readers Teacher's Guide: Emergent*   31

Stage A Book 5
Five Birds and Five Mice

Learning About	Five
Strand	Number
Focus	Counting groups to five
Additional Concepts	Prediction, positional vocabulary

Links with other PM Books
Where are the sunhats? (PM Level 6)
A birthday cake for Ben (PM Level 3)
Cat and Mouse (PM Plus Starters 2)

About the Book
An illustrated fictional story based on counting and grouping mixed sets to a sum of five.

Mathematical language	High-frequency words	Numerals
one, two, three, four, five, little, in, up	are, can, comes, go, here, is, no, oh, the, to, where	1, 2, 3, 4, 5

Focusing on the concept

- *Cover and title page:* Focus on the number five as a group of five birds or mice. Look for groups of five objects in the classroom. Children can count five digits on each hand, or sit in rows of five. Discuss the icon on the title page – five as a numeral, a word, and a dot pattern.

- *Pages 2–15:* Connect the number words in the text with the numerals and the groups of birds and mice. Focus on the concept that the number of five animals remains constant even though positions and groupings change. Make number stories using different groupings of the birds and mice, such as on page 8: *One mouse is looking at the cat; four mice are not looking at the cat.*

- *Page 16:* Using the picture, make number stories as above, but using three or more addends.

Reinforcing the concept

- Use counters to make groupings to a sum of five. Write statements on labels, such as *4 green counters and 1 yellow counter.*

- Reverse the addends and observe that the statements are still true.

- Discuss **zero** as an addend.

Discovering additional concepts

- **Prediction:** Before reading the book with the children, encourage them to discuss each picture in order, and to predict events that may occur on the following page.

- **Positional vocabulary:** Discuss the words **on**, **up**, **down**, **in**, **out** and **to** as they relate to the text. Read *Cat and Mouse* (**over**, **under**) and *Can you see the Eggs?* (PM Level 2).

Using the blackline masters

1. Read the verse and color the pictures. Trace and complete the numerals, words, and pattern.

2. Trace over the gray words and numerals, and color the pictures. Write the correct words and numerals in the spaces.

3. Trace over the gray words. Draw birds and mice in positions that make the statements true. Add numerals in spaces.

Name _____

Five Birds and Five Mice

Look out, five birds!

And five mice, too!

The hungry cat

is after you!

5	5	5	___	___
five	five	five	_____	_____

Five Birds and Five Mice © Rigby, 2004.
This page may be photocopied for educational use within the purchasing institution.

Blackline master 1 *Rigby PM Math Readers Teacher's Guide: Emergent* 33

Name _____

Here are five birds.

One, two, three, four, five birds.

  1   2   3   4   5

Here are five mice.

One, two, three, four, five mice.

  1   2   3   4   5

I can see five cats.

One, _____, _____, _____, _____ cats.

  1   ___   ___   ___   ___

Name _____

Here are five birds.

Two birds are up in the tree.

Three birds are down on the grass.

2 birds and 3 birds.

Here are five mice.

One mouse is in the hole.

Four mice are not in the hole.

____ mice and ____ mouse.

Five Birds and Five Mice © Rigby, 2004.
This page may be photocopied for educational use within the purchasing institution.

Blackline master 3 *Rigby PM Math Readers Teacher's Guide: Emergent*   35

Stage A Book 6
Red Block, Blue Block

Learning About	Two-element patterns
Strand	Number
Focus	Two-element repeating patterns
Additional Concepts	Counting, positioning

Links with other PM Books
Days of the Week (Rigby PM Math Readers Stage A)
Billy Can Count (Rigby PM Plus Level 6)
Party Hat Patterns (Rigby PM Math Readers Stage B)

About the Book
Using small red and blue blocks, two children form a two-element repeating pattern based on color change.

Mathematical language	High-frequency words	Numerals
one, five, patterns	and, are, at, can, go, goes, here, it, look, said, see, the, this, red, blue	1, 5

Focusing on the concept

- *Cover and title page:* Predict what the children might be going to do with the blocks. Use the title page icon as a guide. Introduce the word **pattern** and discuss the procedure for forming a pattern.
- *Pages 2–5:* Read aloud the text, then ask the children how they can check that the statements are correct (counting).
- *Pages 6–15:* Connect the text with the patterning procedure. Before turning each page, ask the children to predict who will have the next turn, and what color the block will be.
- *Page 16:* Use classroom blocks to form the patterns shown, and to make different patterns.

Reinforcing the concept

- Using a variety of materials, such as beads or geometric shapes, the children can form two-element patterns by making color and shape changes. These patterns can be formed horizontally or vertically.

Discovering additional concepts

- **Counting:** Count the decreasing groups of blocks in front of the children. Introduce the subtraction procedure, using the words **take away**. Use the term **zero** on page 15.
- **Positioning:** Use a variety of classroom materials to make similar patterns. Comment on the fact that the pattern remains constant when "read" from either end.

Using the blackline masters

1. Read the verse and color the shapes red and blue.
2. Color the shapes in the colors stated. Complete the shapes on the spaces provided.
3. Complete the patterns, then color the shapes in the colors stated.

Name _____

Rigby PM Math Readers

Red Block, Blue Block

We made a pattern with the blocks...
red for me, and blue for you.
We put them in a long, long line...
red and blue and red and blue.

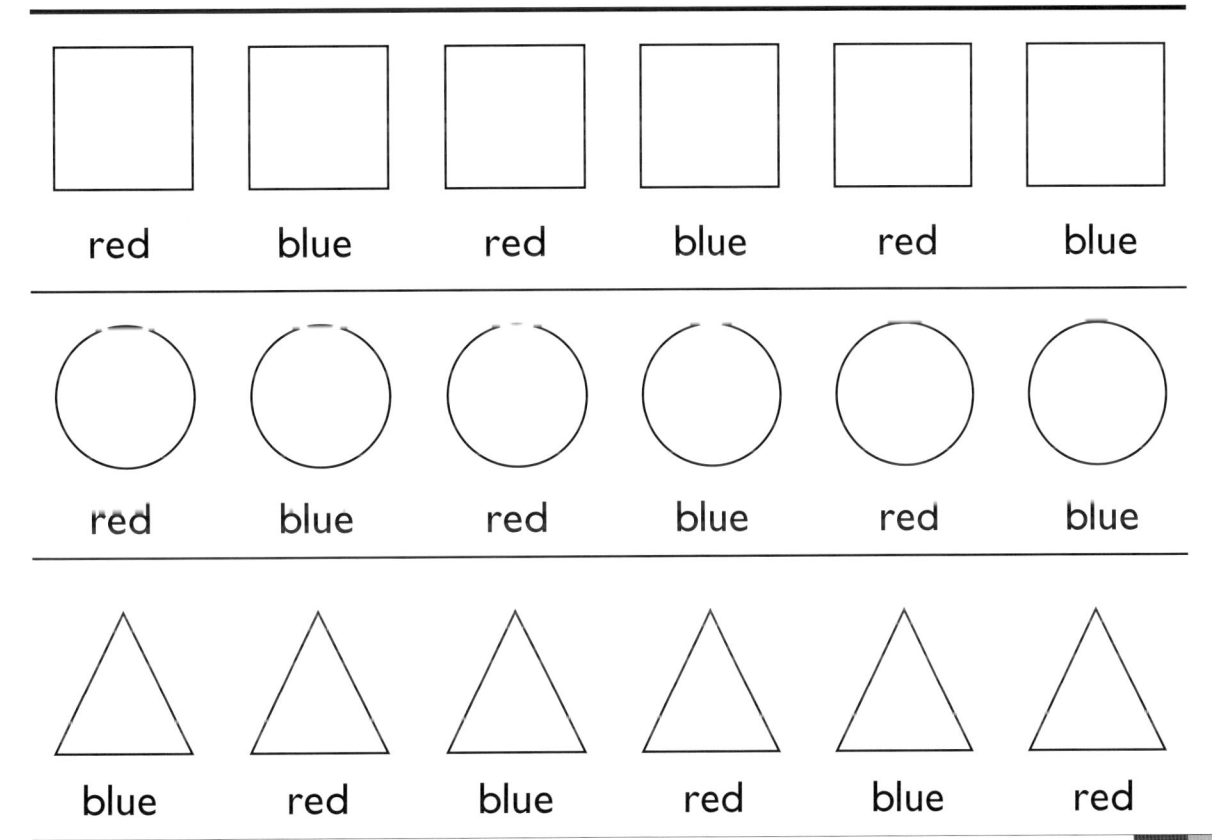

| red | blue | red | blue | red | blue |

| red | blue | red | blue | red | blue |

| blue | red | blue | red | blue | red |

Red Block, Blue Block © Rigby, 2004.
This page may be photocopied for educational use within the purchasing institution.

Blackline master 1 *Rigby PM Math Readers Teacher's Guide: Emergent* 37

Name _____

This pattern goes red, yellow, red, yellow, red, yellow.

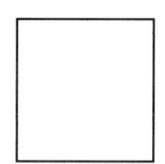

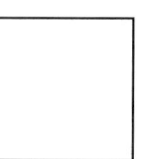

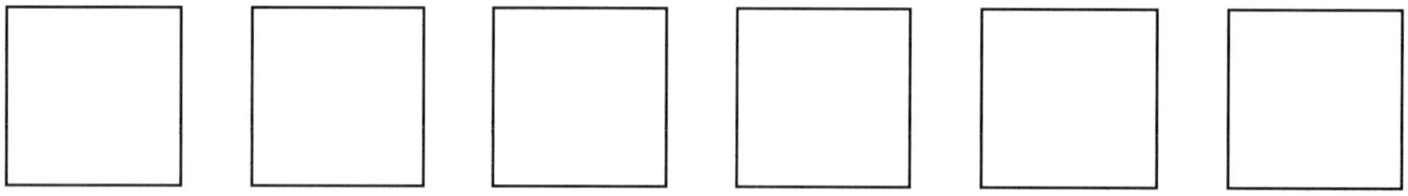

This pattern goes blue, green, blue, green, blue, green.

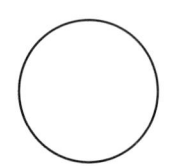

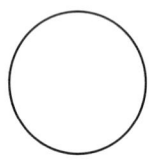

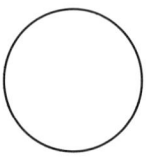

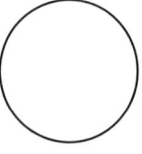

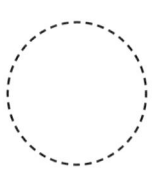

This pattern goes green, yellow, green, yellow, green, yellow.

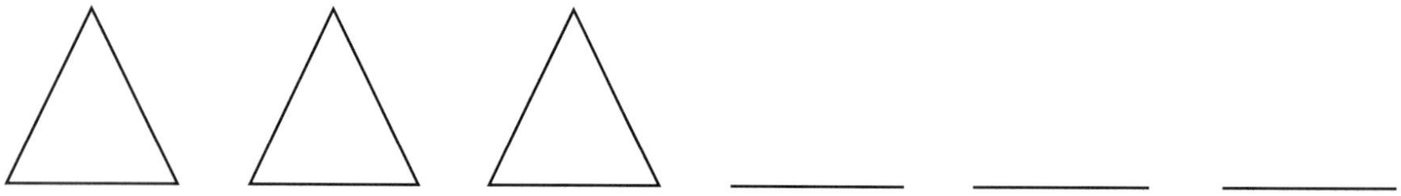

Name _____

Rigby PM Math Readers

This pattern goes blue, red, blue, red, blue, red.

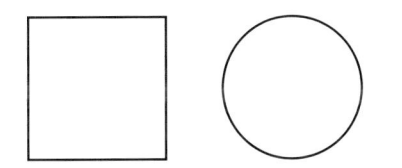

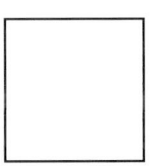

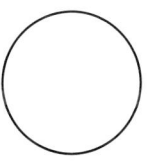

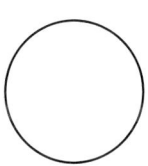

This pattern goes yellow, blue, yellow, blue, yellow, blue.

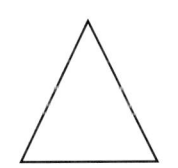

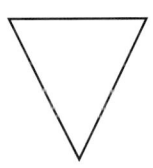

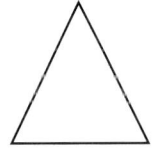

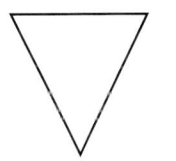

This pattern goes red, green, red, green, red, green.

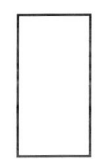

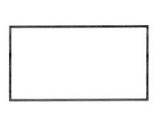

Red Block, Blue Block © Rigby, 2004.
This page may be photocopied for educational use within the purchasing institution.

Blackline master 3 *Rigby PM Math Readers Teacher's Guide: Emergent*

Stage A Book 7
Counting Down

Learning About Strand Groups
Focus Number
Additional Concepts Groups in descending order
Sequencing, grouping

Links with other PM Books
Seven little ducks (PM Readalongs)
Over in the meadow (PM Readalongs)
Sorting Leaves (Rigby PM Math Readers Stage A)

About the Book
A child visits a pet shop and counts groups of animals, in descending order, from six birds down to one kitten.

Mathematical language	High-frequency words	Numerals
one, two, three, four, five, six	am, at, can, I, like, looking, see, the	1, 2, 3, 4, 5, 6

Focusing on the concept

- *Cover and title page:* Establish the children's prior knowledge of counting down/backward. Reinforce this concept by studying the groups of animals on the cover, and connect these groups with the dot patterns on the title page.
- *Pages 2–3:* Name and count the total for each group. Write the children's responses on a chalkboard, for example *We can see 6 birds.*
- *Pages 4–15:* Discuss order when counting backward. Predict, check, and confirm the group that will come next.
- *Page 16:* Review the counting backward sequence. Reinforce order and position by identifying the numbers that come **after, before,** and **between.** Ask questions that require the children to count backward.

Reinforcing the concept

- On the floor, place large cards with pictures or numerals 1–6 on them. Count aloud backward from 6 while a child walks on each card as this number is called out. Extend to pictures and numerals 1–10.
- Practice the counting backward using the book *Seven little ducks.*

Discovering additional concepts

- **Sequencing:** Have the children sit in a circle. Have a child begin to count backward and continue the counting around the circle. Ask: *"Who do you think will say 2?"*
- **Grouping:** Make "stairs" with stacking blocks. Count the groups both forward and backward. Introduce **zero** in its position in the counting sequence.

Using the blackline masters

1. Read the verse and color the pictures. Trace and complete the numerals, words, and pattern.
2. Review numerical order when counting backward. Trace and complete the numerals, words, and patterns.
3. Cut out the pictures. Glue onto each strip of paper in descending order. Glue the numerals and words under the appropriate pictures.

Name _____

Counting Down

In the pet shop it is fun, counting down from six to one.

6	5	4	___	___	___
six	five	four	___	___	___

Counting Down © Rigby, 2004.
This page may be photocopied for educational use within the purchasing institution.

Blackline master 1 *Rigby PM Math Readers Teacher's Guide: Emergent*

Name _____

●● ●● ●● ●● ●● ●
●● ●● ●● ●● ●●
●● ●● ●● ●

| 6 | 5 | ___ | 3 | ___ | ___ |

| ▢▢ ▢▢ ▢▢ | | ▢▢ ▢▢ | | ▢▢ | |

| 6 | ___ | 4 | ___ | 2 | ___ |

| △△ △△ △△ | △△ △△ △ | | | △△ | |

| six | five | four | three | two | one |

Name _____

Rigby
PM Math
Readers

Provide large sheets of construction paper that have been folded into 6 equal spaces.

| 1 | 2 | 3 | 4 | 5 | 6 |

| one | two | three | four | five | six |

Counting Down © Rigby, 2004.
This page may be photocopied for educational use within the purchasing institution.

Blackline master 3 *Rigby PM Math Readers Teacher's Guide: Emergent* 43

Stage A Book 8
Big Shapes and Little Shapes

Learning About : Shapes
Strand : Shape and space
Focus : Recognizing two-dimensional shapes
Additional Concepts : Color, comparison

Links with other PM Books
A Game with Shapes (Rigby PM Math Readers Stage A)
Here come the shapes (Rigby PM Plus Level 6)
Big and little (PM Plus Starters 2)

About the Book
Using circles, squares, triangles, and rectangles, two children show differences in size and shape.

Mathematical language	High-frequency words	Numeral
one, two, circle, square, triangle, rectangle, big, little	and, at, can, is, look, see, the, we red, blue, yellow, green,	2

Focusing on the concept

- *Cover and title page:* Name the shapes, and describe them by size and color. Ask the children to point to specific shapes, and then to describe them. Discuss the properties of the shapes, such as sides, or corners.
- *Pages 2–5:* After reading the text, focus on the word **circle.** Ask the children to find this word in the text, and to connect the word with the shape in the picture. Note that **one** and **one** are addends for **two.**
- *Pages 6–15:* Connect the words **square, triangle,** and **rectangle** with the shapes in the picture.
- *Page 16:* Use this page to reinforce the shape names, and also to reinforce the additional concepts

Reinforcing the concept

- Use the shape names to identify a variety of two-dimensional shapes in the classroom, for example, *Can you see a big blue rectangle?*
- Put a variety of two-dimensional shapes into a bag and ask children, in turn, to find a specified shape using the sense of touch.

Discovering additional concepts

- **Color:** Focus on the different color names in the text. With the book open at page 3, ask the children to name a group of red items, such as a red pencil/block, j etc.
- **Comparison:** Discuss the differences in size, shape, and color. Find the words **big** and **little** in the text. Use the PM books listed above to compare size, color, and shape.

Using the blackline masters

1. Read the verse and color the pictures. Trace over the gray words. Color the shapes to match those in the book.
2. Trace over the gray words, and color the shapes to match the statements.
3. Add the missing words to the spaces. Color the shapes to match the statements.

Rigby PM Math Readers Teacher's Guide: Emergent

Name _____

Big Shapes and Little Shapes

Big and little circles...

big and little squares...

triangles and rectangles...

they all go up here.

Two red circles

Two blue squares

Two yellow triangles

Two green rectangles

Big Shapes and Little Shapes © Rigby, 2004.
This page may be photocopied for educational use within the purchasing institution.

Name _____

I can see two red circles.

One circle is little.

One circle is big.

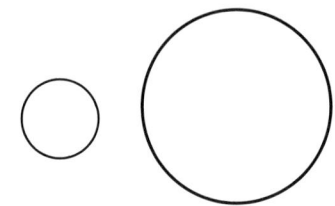

I can see two blue squares.

One square is little.

One square is big.

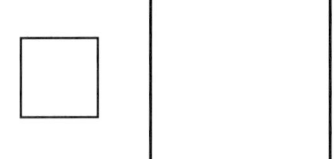

I can see

a little yellow triangle

and a big green rectangle.

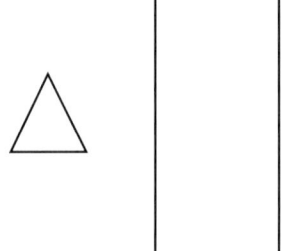

Name _____

A big red circle

A little yellow triangle

A little red _____

A ____ green rectangle

A ____ yellow triangle

A _____ blue square

A ____ red square

A ____ green _____

Stage A Book 9
A Game with Shapes

Learning About	Position, direction, and movement
Strand	Shape and space
Focus	Following instructions
Additional Concepts	Shape, color, and size

Links with other PM Books
Big Shapes and Little Shapes (Rigby PM Math Readers Stage A)
Shapes with a Rope (Rigby PM Math Readers Stage B)
A roof and a door (PM Nonfiction Levels 5/6)

About the Book
Two children play a game using large shapes painted on concrete: circles, rectangles, squares, and triangles.

Mathematical language
circle, rectangle, square, triangle, big, little, in

High-frequency words
am, are, at, go, I, in, look, me, said, the, to, we,
blue, green, red, yellow

Focusing on the concept

- *Cover and title page:* Name the shapes painted on the concrete and describe them by color and size. Recognize that the color of each shape in the title page icon matches those painted on the concrete, i.e. all the circles are red.
- *Pages 2–5:* Introduce vocabulary that distinguishes one shape from another, for example, number of sides.
- *Pages 6–15:* Use picture clues to predict the instructions. Read aloud the text to check and confirm.
- *Page 16:* Make sure the children understand how the arrows indicate the path taken by each child. Encourage discussion, such as *First Kate was in the big yellow triangle, then she....* Use this page to reinforce the names of these shapes, and discuss their properties.

Reinforcing the concept

- Draw colored shapes on concrete. Have children give each other directions.
- Make some large cards with arrows painted on them. Use the arrows as non-verbal instructions.

Discovering additional concepts

- **Shape and color:** Provide a variety of shapes made from plastic or felt for the children to sort by shape and color.
- **Size:** Play this game: Sit the children in pairs, one behind the other. The front child puts his/her hands behind his/her back. The child at the back places two same shapes of different sizes into the other child's hands and asks for one of the shapes, for example, *Give me the big circle.*

Using the blackline masters

1. Read the verse and color the picture. Trace around the shapes and color them.
2. Trace over the gray words. Color the shapes. Cut out each bear and glue inside a shape.
3. Name the shapes and count how many of each have been used to make the train. Write the answers in the spaces. Color the train picture.

Name _____

Rigby PM Math Readers

A Game with Shapes

Look at all the colored shapes,

painted on the ground.

Some have sides and corners,

some of them are round.

red triangles	△	△	△
green squares	▢	▢	▢
blue rectangles	▭	▭	▭
yellow circles	○	○	○

A Game with Shapes © Rigby, 2004.
This page may be photocopied for educational use within the purchasing institution.

Blackline master 1 *Rigby PM Math Readers Teacher's Guide: Emergent*

Name _____

Teddy is in

the big red circle.

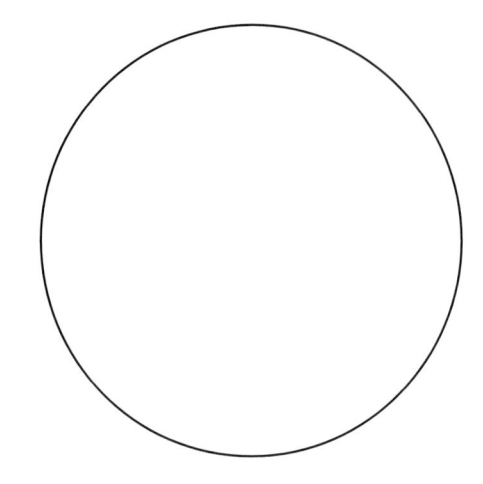

Teddy is in

the big blue rectangle.

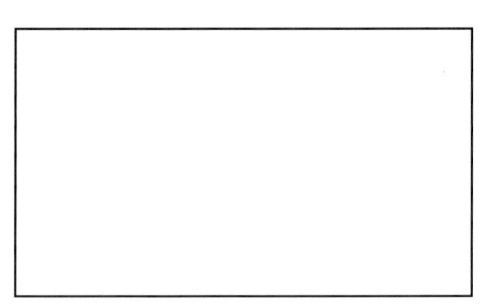

Teddy is in

the little yellow square.

Name _____

Rigby
PM Math Readers

1	2	3	4	5	6
one	two	three	four	five	six

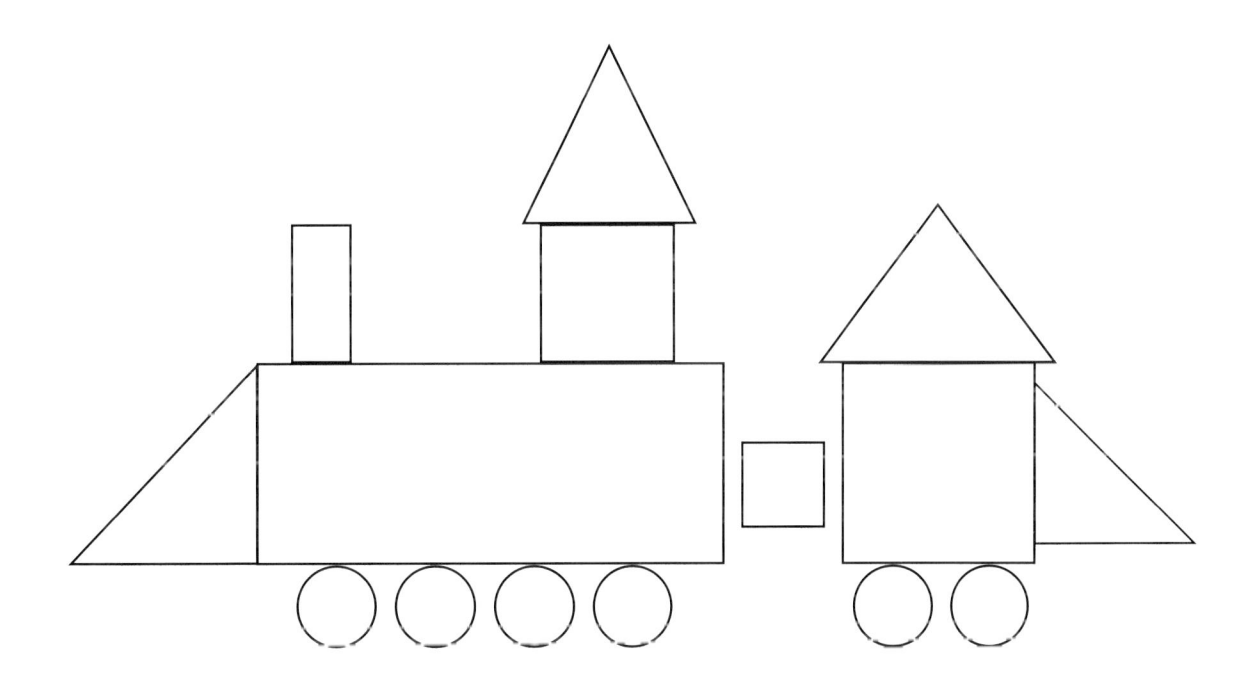

I can see _____ circles. ◯

I can see _____ squares. ☐

I can see _____ triangles. △

I can see _____ rectangles. ▭

A Game with Shapes © Rigby, 2004.
This page may be photocopied for educational use within the purchasing institution.

Blackline master 3 *Rigby PM Math Readers Teacher's Guide: Emergent* 51

Stage A Book 10
Making a Butterfly

Learning About Symmetry
Strand Shape and space
Focus Making a symmetrical design
Additional Concepts Sequencing, color

Links with other PM Books
Making a bird (PM Nonfiction Level 2)
Making a rabbit (PM Nonfiction Level 2)
Making a dinosaur (PM Nonfiction Level 2)

About the Book
A child learns how to follow a procedure, and to use shape and color to make a symmetrical design.

Mathematical language	High-frequency words
one, same	a, am, and, are, at, go, going, here, I, is, like, look, my, on, the, this, to red, blue, yellow,

Focusing on the concept

- *Cover and title page:* Focus on the completed butterfly, and discuss the preliminary procedures of drawing, folding, and cutting.
- *Pages 2–3:* Ask the children to predict what the girl might be going to do to achieve the result that is shown on the cover.
- *Pages 4–5:* Check the children's statements from the previous page against the text.
- *Pages 6–11:* Make connections with the name of the color and the picture. Note that the girl makes one blue dot, two red dots, and three yellow dots.
- *Pages 12–15:* Discuss reasons for completing this stage of the procedure carefully.
- *Page 16:* Connect the word **same** with the word **symmetrical.**

Reinforcing the concept

- Discuss whether the same symmetrical result could have been achieved if paint had been put on the left wing.
- Observe symmetry of the children's features.
- Display butterflies on the wall to emphasize a variety of symmetrical designs.

Discovering additional concepts

Sequencing: Explain the reasons for following a sequential procedure in order to achieve a satisfactory result.

Color: Make butterflies with the children. Use a variety of colors and patterns. Observe the effect of overlapping colors to make new colors and textures.

Using the blackline masters

1. Read the verse and color the picture. Color the butterfly in the stated colors.
2. Using this template, follow the procedure outlined in the book to make a butterfly. Use a variety of colors and designs.
3. Color the left wing in the stated colors. Then color the right wing so that both wings are symmetrical.

Rigby PM Math Readers Teacher's Guide: Emergent

Name _____

Rigby PM Math Readers

Making a Butterfly

I cut, I paint, and fold,

and I can tell you why.

I open up the wings...

and look...

I made a butterfly!

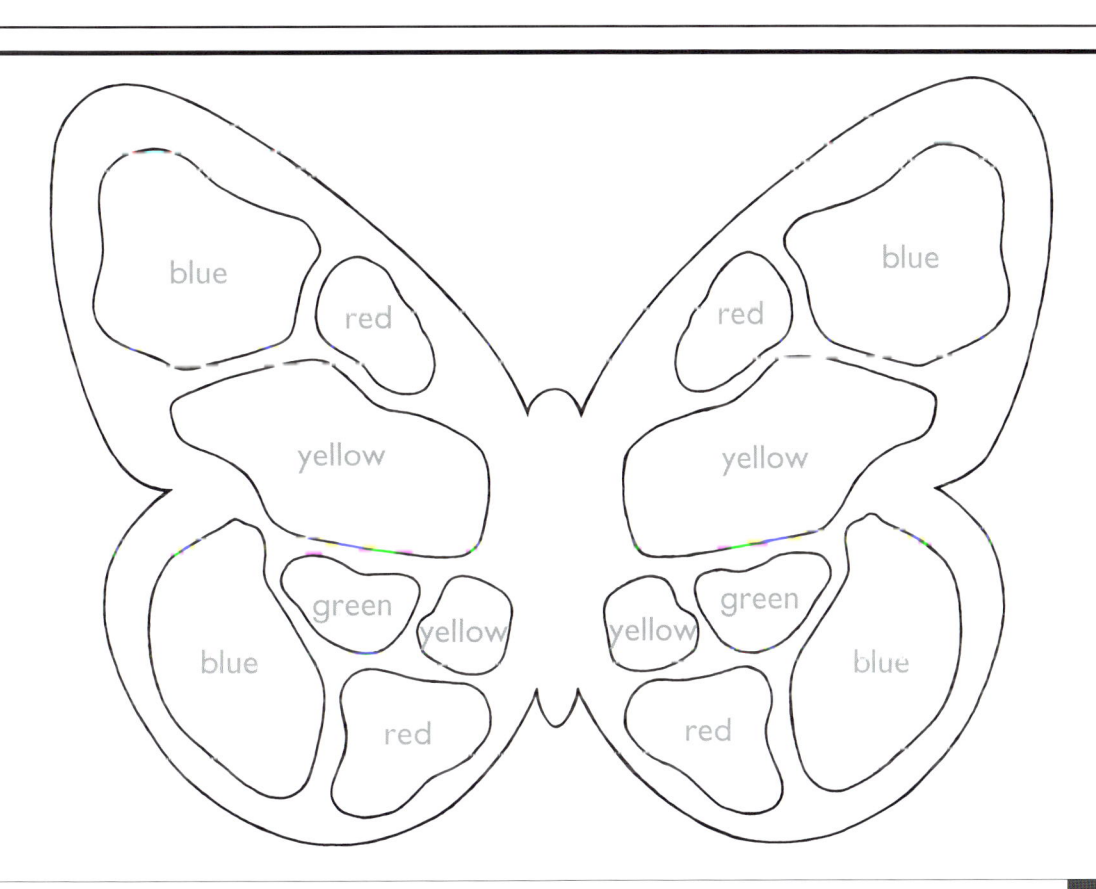

blue   red   red   blue

yellow   yellow

green yellow   yellow green
blue   blue
    red   red

Making a Butterfly © Rigby, 2004.
This page may be photocopied for educational use within the purchasing institution.

Blackline master 1 *Rigby PM Math Readers Teacher's Guide: Emergent*

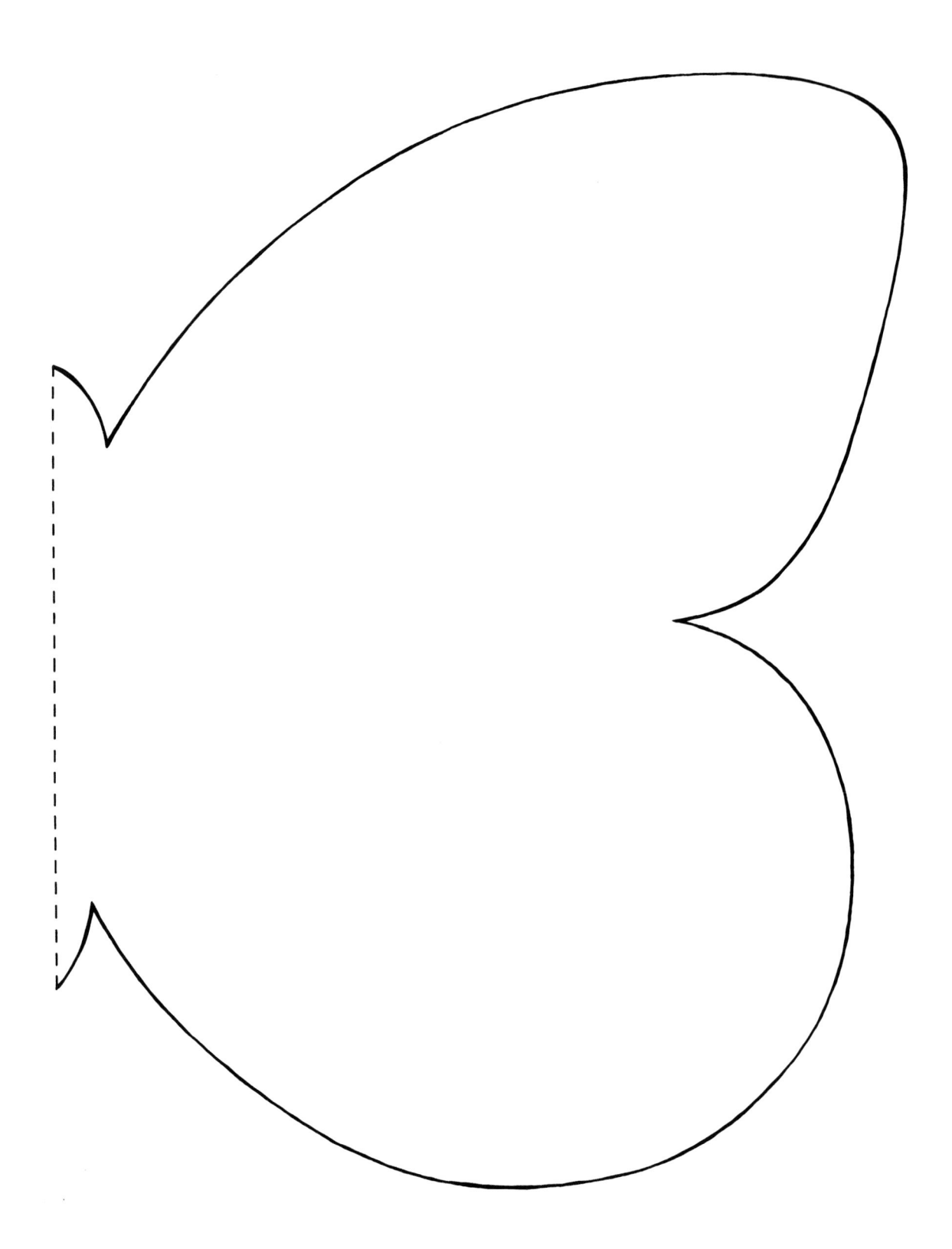

Name _____

Making a Butterfly © Rigby, 2004.
This page may be photocopied for educational use within the purchasing institution.

Blackline master 2 *Rigby PM Math Readers Teacher's Guide: Emergent*

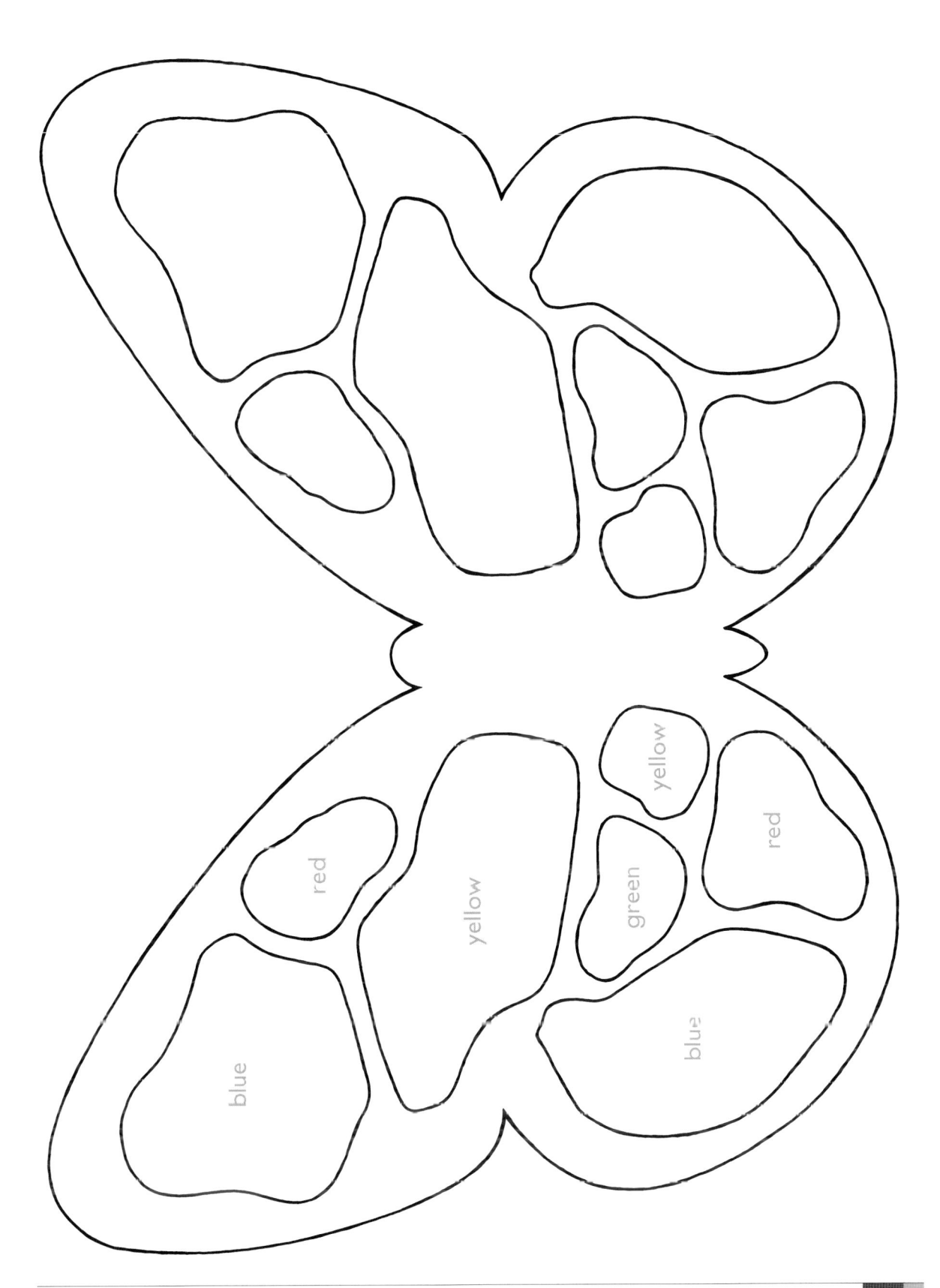

Name _____

Rigby PM Math Readers

Making a Butterfly © Rigby, 2004.
This page may be photocopied for educational use within the purchasing institution.

Blackline master 3 *Rigby PM Math Readers Teacher's Guide: Emergent* 55

Stage A Book 11
Long and Short

Learning About Strand	Length
	Measurement
Focus	Comparison of long and short
Additional Concepts	Movement, positional vocabulary

Links with other PM Books
Four Cars (Rigby PM Maths Readers Stage A)
Tall things (PM Nonfiction Levels 5/6)
The Toytown rescue (PM Plus Level 5)

About the Book
Two children each make a road with building blocks. One road is long, the other is short. The children take a toy car along their road to a garage.

Mathematical language
long, short, on, under

High-frequency words
a, at, goes, going, is, it, look, my, said, the, this, to, too, went, red, blue

Focusing on the concept

- *Cover and title page:* Connect the title with the length of the two roads. Compare the blocks in the icon to reinforce understanding of **long** and **short**.
- *Pages 2–5:* Talk about the path made by the long road using words like **along, around,** and **under**.
- *Pages 6–15:* Reinforce movement and directional vocabulary. Talk about the construction of the short road, such as fewer blocks, goes straight to the garage, etc.
- *Page 16:* On a chalkboard, list the names of objects that the children suggest are **long**. Make another list of objects that are **short**. Compare the lengths of related classroom objects, such as a long rope/pencil and a short rope/pencil.

Reinforcing the concept

- Put pairs of objects that differ only by length into a "*long and short*" box, such as two blocks. Write the headings *Long* and *Short* on a chart, and sort the objects under the headings.
- Find objects that are about the same length as a given object. First estimate if they are the same length and then check by measuring. Focus on the procedure for measuring.

Discovering additional concepts

- **Movement:** Have children build roads from building blocks. The children can give one another instructions for moving an object along the roads.
- **Positional vocabulary:** Reinforce the words **on** and **under**. Introduce other vocabulary, such as **around, between, over,** and **behind**.

Using the blackline masters

1. Read the verse and color the picture. Trace over the gray words. Draw blocks in the spaces.
2. Distinguish between long and short, and between the colors. Color the item that illustrates the statement.
3. Trace over the gray words. Compare the pictures. Put the correct word in each space.

Name _____

Long and short

The long road is for me.

The short road is for you.

My little car is red,

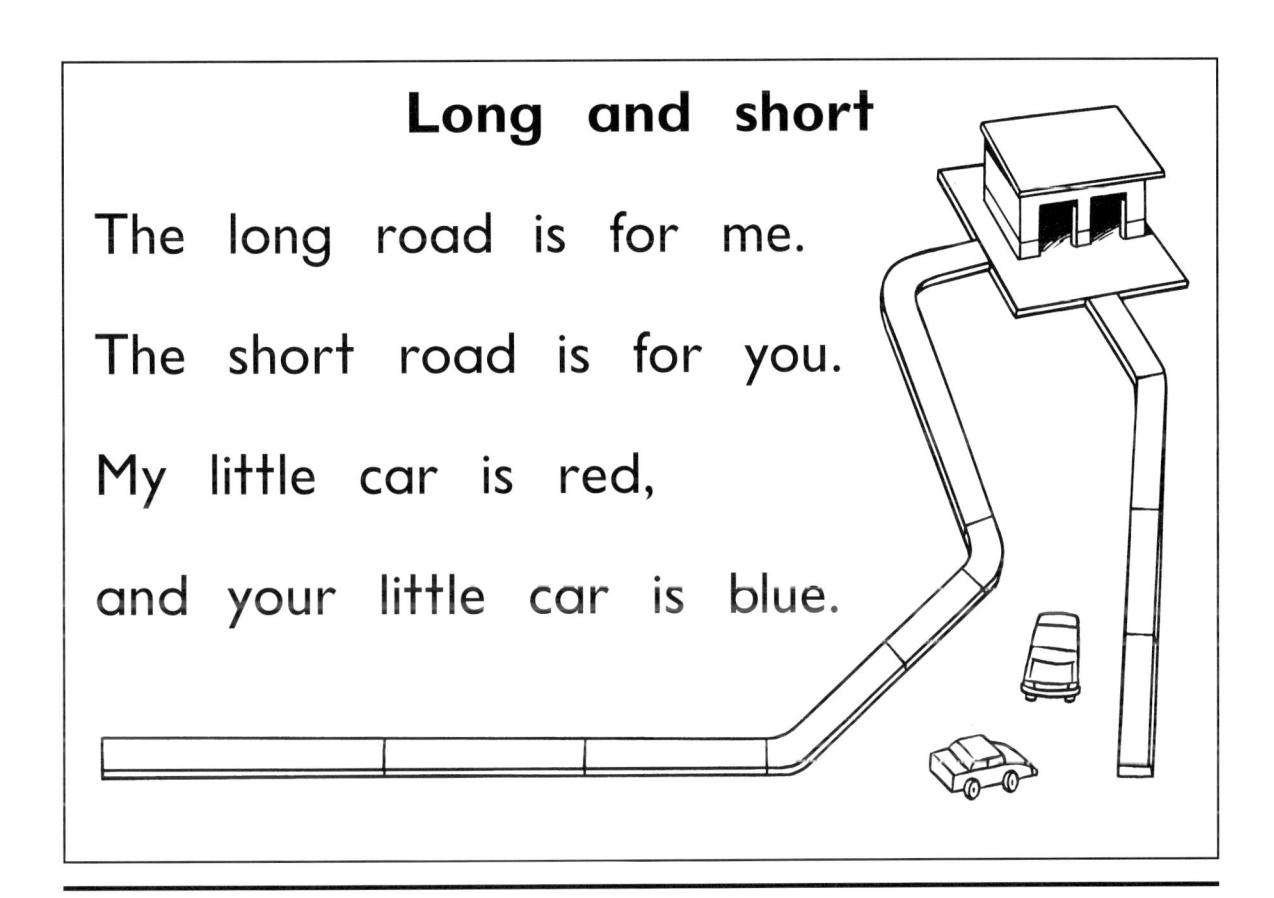

and your little car is blue.

| long | short |

This is a long block.

This is a short block.

Name _____

Rigby PM Math Readers

The long pencil is red.	The short ribbon is blue.
The long snake is green.	The short paintbrush is yellow.

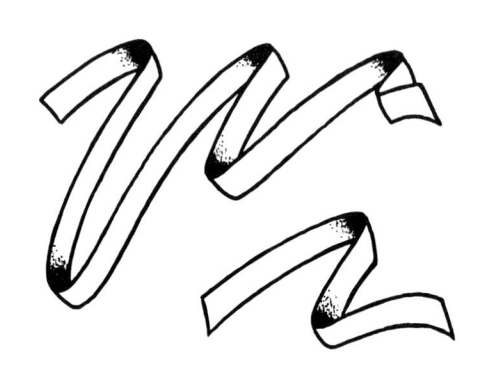

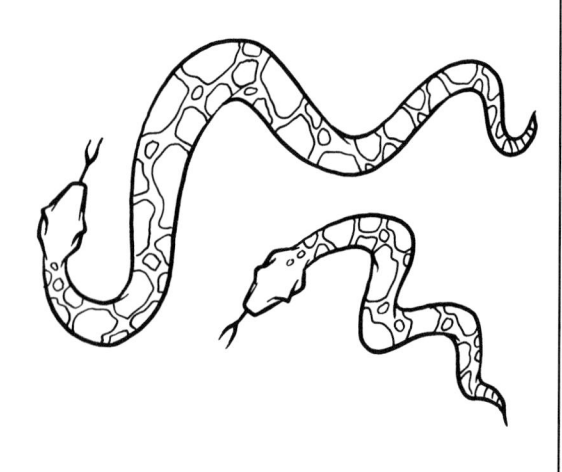

Name _____

PM Math Readers

| long | | short |

Look at the long road.

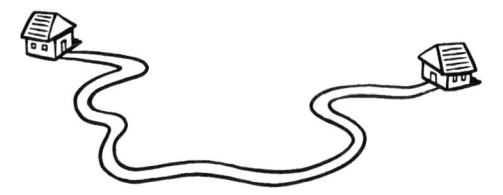

Look at the short road.

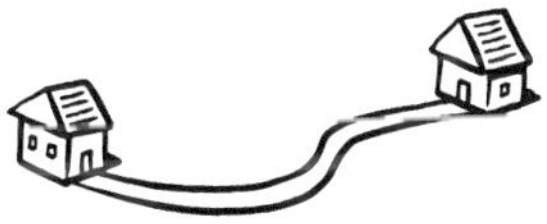

Look at the _____ train.

Look at the _____ train.

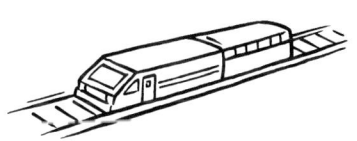

Look at the _____ bridge.

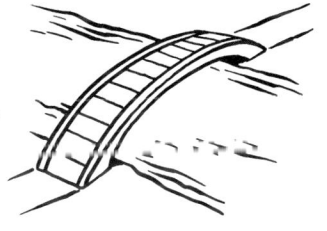

Look at the _____ bridge.

Long and Short © Rigby, 2004.
This page may be photocopied for educational use within the purchasing institution.

Blackline master 3 *Rigby PM Math Readers Teacher's Guide: Emergent* 59

Stage A Book 12
Sorting Leaves

Learning About	Classification
Strand	Data
Focus	Classifying by color
Additional Concepts	Sorting, grouping

Links with other PM Books
Counting Down (Rigby PM Math Readers Stage A)
Animal Graphs (Rigby PM Math Readers Stage B)
Red and blue and yellow (PM Nonfiction Levels 5/6)

About the Book
Three children gather leaves and sort them into three groups according to color. The leaves are arranged in a simple horizontal graph format.

Mathematical language	High-frequency words	Numerals
one, two, three, four, five	and, are, at, for, go, here, look, looking, my, on, the, this, we, green, red, yellow	1, 2, 3, 4, 5

Focusing on the concept

- *Cover and title page:* Discuss sorting by size, color, or shape as options for forming groups. Predict how the leaves might be sorted. Connect the colors of the leaves with the leaves in the icon.
- *Pages 2–9:* Read and discuss the text. Begin to recognize how many leaves are in each group without counting.
- *Pages 10–15:* Reinforce one-to-one correspondence as the leaves are arranged on the grid, such as one space, one leaf. Read the labels and discuss their function.
- *Page 16:* Discuss the features of this type of visual presentation, such as the ordered array of data. Use the words **more than** and **fewer than** as the number of leaves in each group is compared. Explain that keeping the leaves in a line makes the counting easier.

Reinforcing the concept

Compare two or three sets of data in simple graph form, for example, favorite ice-cream flavors. Compare verbally using words such as **more, less, fewer,** and **same.** Present data visually using both horizontal and vertical formats.

Discovering additional concepts

- **Sorting:** Read aloud stories that provide opportunities for sorting and matching, such as *Goldilocks and the Three Bears*.
- **Grouping:** Put objects that can be sorted by color, shape, or size into a container. Sort the objects into groups. Talk about why the members of each group belong together. Compare using appropriate vocabulary, such as *There are more…*; *There are fewer…*.

Using the blackline masters

1. Read the verse and color the picture. Trace over the numerals and color the leaves.
2. Read the labels. Trace over the leaf shapes and color appropriately. Trace over the gray words.
3. Read the labels and count cars required. Color and cut out the cars. Glue into position on the graph.

Name _____

Sorting leaves

Look at all the leaves!

They have fallen from the tree.

Red, yellow, green…

Five, four, three…

red leaves	1	2	3	4	5
yellow leaves	1	2	3	4	
green leaves	1	2	3		

Sorting Leaves © Rigby, 2004.
This page may be photocopied for educational use within the purchasing institution.

Name _____

green leaves	1	2	3	4	5
red leaves	1	2	3	4	
yellow leaves	1	2	3		

Here are five green leaves.

Here are four red leaves.

Here are three yellow leaves.

Name _____

5		
4	4	
3	3	3
2	2	2
1	1	1
yellow cars	green cars	red cars

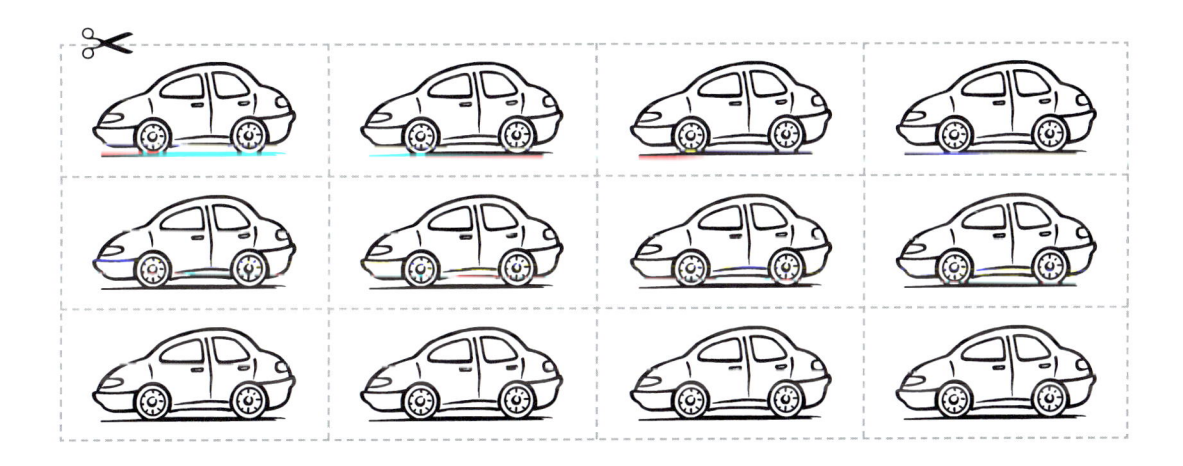

Stage B Book 1
Days of the Week

Learning About	Time
Strand	Measurement/Time
Focus	The days of the week in order
Additional Concepts	Difference: weekdays and weekends, mathematical activities

Links with other PM Books
Fishing (PM Starters 2)
Animal Graphs (Rigby PM Math Readers Stage B)
One More Frog (Rigby PM Math Readers Stage C)

About the Book
A child makes statements about a math-based activity on each of the weekdays and a family-based activity on each of the weekend days.

Mathematical language

one, Monday, Tuesday, Wednesday, Thursday, Friday, Saturday, Sunday, big, long, under, into, pattern, shapes

High-frequency words

all, do, playing, reading, school, some, this, today, with, yellow, red, green, blue

Focusing on the concept

- *Cover and title page:* Read the days of the week in order. Differentiate between **weekdays** and the **weekend.** Count the number of days that are school days and the number that are the weekend days. Ask questions to establish the children's prior knowledge. Use their responses to guide discussion while the text is being read.

- *Pages 2–11:* Discuss the mathematical activities in the photographs. Connect the names of the days with activities that the children do at school. Make sure the children understand the repeated sequence of the days throughout the week.

- *Pages 12–15:* Connect the events in the photographs to weekend activities. Ask questions like: "How do you know this is not a school day?" and "What did you do last Sunday?"

- *Page 16:* Reinforce children's understanding of the order of the days by using the words **yesterday, today,** and **tomorrow.**

Reinforcing the concept

- Read aloud stories that reinforce the order of the days of the week, such as *The Very Hungry Caterpillar* (Eric Carle, Hamish Hamilton, 1969).

- Keep a daily weather chart.

Discovering the additional concepts

- **Difference (weekdays/weekend):** Make a booklet about everyday activities that happen on **weekdays** and another about the **weekend** days. Read and compare.

- **Mathematical activities:** Write the days of the week in order on a chart. Make a set of labels: *yesterday, today, tomorrow.* Connect math activities that the class has been doing, or are about to do, with the days. Place the labels beside the appropriate days on the chart.

Using the blackline masters

1. Read the verse and color the picture. Trace over the gray words. Write the names of the days again in the spaces.

2. Copy the blackline master onto colored heavy paper. Cut out each card. Place in the correct order starting with different days.

3. Reinforce order using **today, yesterday,** and **tomorrow.** Write the names of the days.

Rigby PM Math Readers Teacher's Guide: Emergent

Name _____

Rigby PM Math Readers

Monday, Tuesday, Wednesday…

Thursday, Friday, too.

They are the days I go to school

and I learn something new.

Monday	
Tuesday	
Wednesday	
Thursday	
Friday	
Saturday	
Sunday	

Days of the Week © Rigby, 2004.
This page may be photocopied for educational use within the purchasing institution.

Blackline master 1 *Rigby PM Math Readers Teacher's Guide: Emergent*

Name _____

Monday

Tuesday

Wednesday

Thursday

Friday

Saturday

Sunday

Name _____

Rigby PM Math Readers

Today is Tuesday.

Yesterday was Monday.

Tomorrow will be Wednesday.

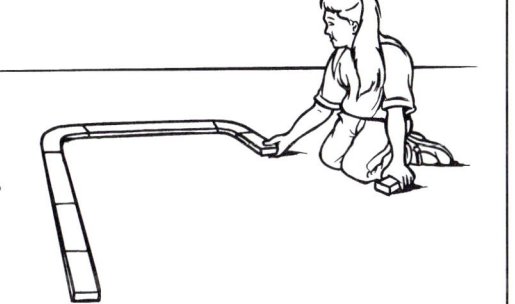

Today is Friday.

Yesterday was _____ .

Tomorrow will be _____ .

Today is _____ .

Yesterday was Saturday.

Tomorrow will be _____ .

Days of the Week © Rigby, 2004.
This page may be photocopied for educational use within the purchasing institution.

Blackline master 3 *Rigby PM Math Readers Teacher's Guide: Emergent* 67

Stage B Book 2

As Heavy As

Learning About	Mass
Strand	Measurement
Focus	Comparing weight and size
Additional Concepts	Estimation, confirmation

Links with other PM Books
Big sea animals (PM Plus Level 2)
Big and little (PM Plus Level 2)
Playing with dough (PM Plus Nonfiction 5/6)
Little Bulldozer helps again (PM Level 9 Set B)

About the book
Two children estimate and compare the weight of a ball of dough in relation to three wooden blocks of different sizes, and in relation to an orange.

Mathematical language

too heavy, not as heavy as, as heavy as, small, smaller, big

High-frequency words

again, be, from, got, her, it, made, of, out, school, some, that, this, will, with, your

Focusing on the concept

- *Cover:* Talk about the scale and how it confirms that the ball of dough and the block of wood are the same weight.
- *Title page:* Discuss the blocks of wood and the orange. Estimate which one/s might be the same weight as the ball of dough.
- *Pages 2–11:* Observe how Lee and Sam hold their arms and hands as they estimate the weight of the dough and each block. Talk about the importance of estimating then confirming by checking with the scale.
- *Pages 12–15:* Talk about the weight of an orange compared to the weight of a wooden block. Note the thoughtful look on Sam's face on page 13 as he considers the problem.
- *Page 16:* Make sure the children are clear in their understanding as you read the text and discuss the photos with them.

Reinforcing the concept

- Practice the "estimate and check" procedure using a variety of environmental materials, such as stones, apples, and shoes.
- Fill small sealable plastic bags with sand, water, leaves, etc. Compare the weight of each filled bag with a ball of dough.
- Compare the weight of a cup of wet sand with the weight of a cup of dry sand.

Discovering the additional concepts

- **Estimation:** Make charts or booklets comparing two weights, for example, *An elephant is heavier than a dog*.
- **Confirmation:** Estimate then measure the heights of three children. Draw pictures then write the words *tall, taller, tallest* under each one.

Using the blackline masters

1. Read the poem. Discuss how to draw a scale showing a block and a ball of equal weight.
2. Find objects in the classroom to compare with the weight of an apple and the weights of their school bags. Draw the objects in a scale.
3. Discuss the choices. Complete each sentence.

Name _____

As Heavy As

This block is too heavy.

I will find a block that's small.

Here is the **best** one…

it's as heavy as the ball.

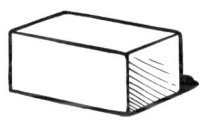

This block is **as heavy as** the ball.

Name _____

A_____

is **as heavy as** an apple.

A _____

is **as heavy as** an apple.

A _____

is **as heavy as** my school bag.

A _____

is **as heavy as** my school bag.

Name _____

Rigby PM Math Readers

A toy car

is **as heavy as** _____ .

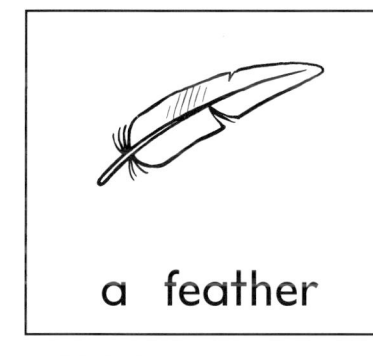

| a feather | an orange | a small block |

A leaf

is **as heavy as** _____ .

| a feather | an orange | a small block |

An elephant
is **as heavy as**
a big truck.

yes   no

As Heavy As © Rigby, 2004.
This page may be photocopied for educational use within the purchasing institution.

Blackline master 3 Rigby PM Math Readers Teacher's Guide: Emergent   71

Stage B Book 3
Shapes with a Rope

Learning About Strand	Formation of shapes
	Shape and Space
Focus	Properties of two-dimensional shapes
Additional Concepts	Prediction, following directions

Links with other PM Books
A Game with Shapes (Rigby PM Math Readers Stage A)
Big Shapes and Little Shapes (Rigby PM Math Readers Stage A)
Here come the shapes (PM Plus Level 6)

About the Book
Groups of children use a long rope to form a variety of large shapes, noting that one child is needed for each corner of the shapes.

Mathematical language	High-frequency words	Numerals
two, four, shape, line, long, big, triangle, square, rectangle, hexagon	children, have, help, like, made, make, new, our, put, some, this, will, with	2, 3, 4, 6

Focusing on the concept

- *Cover and title page:* Name the shape that the children have formed in the cover picture, and count the number of sides and corners the shape has. Locate other hexagons in the classroom and compare. Discuss the procedure for using a rope to form shapes. Name the shapes on the title page, and discuss how many children would be needed to form these shapes.

- *Pages 2–5:* Introduce the setting and discuss the properties of a line. Discuss how the children might be going to form the triangle.

- *Pages 6–15:* Predict how each shape will be formed, and confirm these predictions on the following pages. Connect the names of the shapes with the pictures.

- *Page 16:* Name the properties of each shape and relate to the number of children that are required.

Reinforcing the concept

Use a rope to form shapes outside or on the classroom floor. In each case, ask one child to name the shape to be formed, and then to select the correct number of children required to form that shape. Reinforce the properties of each shape.

Discovering additional concepts

- **Prediction:** Before turning each page, ask the children to predict and describe how the next shape will be formed.

- **Following directions:** In the procedure described in "Reinforcing the concept", the selected child will give directions and the other children can follow these directions to form the requested shapes.

Using the blackline masters

1. Read the verse and color the picture. Trace over the gray words. Fill in the correct number in the space. Draw a child at each corner of each rope shape.

2. Trace over the gray numerals and words. Complete the missing sides on the square and hexagon.

3. Trace over the gray words. Write the correct numbers in the spaces.

Name _____

Shapes with a Rope

Three can make a triangle.

Four can make a square.

Six can make a hexagon.

Look down here!

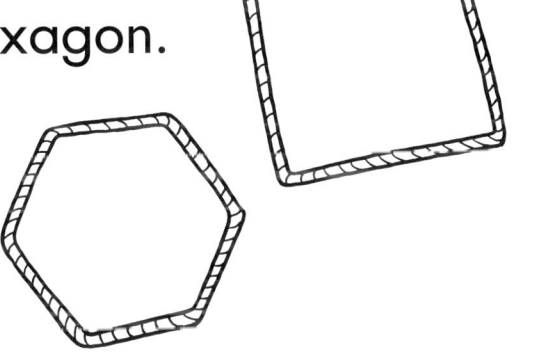

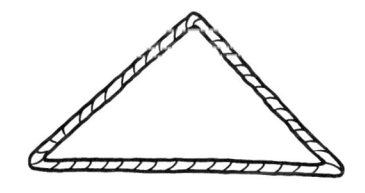

A triangle: __ children

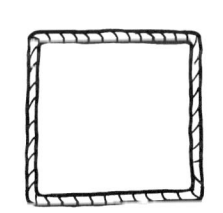

A square: __ children

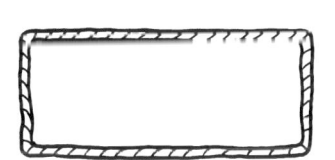

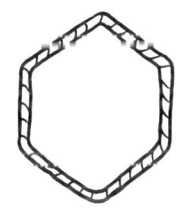

A rectangle: __ children

A hexagon: __ children

Shapes with a Rope © Rigby, 2004.
This page may be photocopied for educational use within the purchasing institution.

Blackline master 1 *Rigby PM Math Readers Teacher's Guide: Emergent*

Name _____

2 children
can make
a line.

3 children
can make
a triangle.

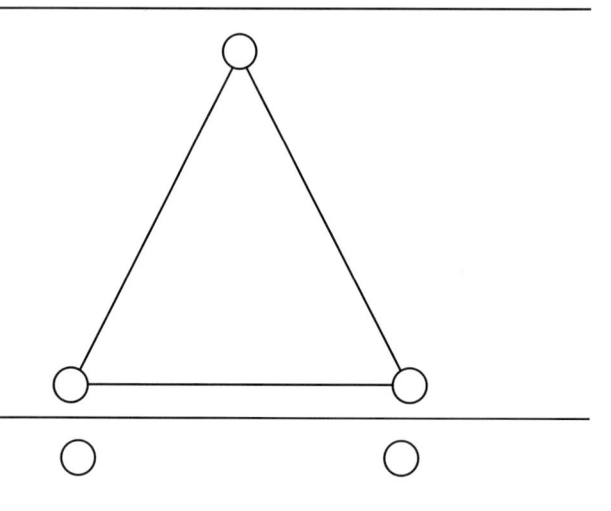

4 children
can make
a square.

6 children
can make
a hexagon.

Name _____

The triangle has 3 sides and 3 corners.

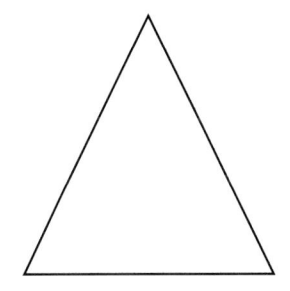

The square has ___ sides and ___ corners.

The rectangle has ___ sides and ___ corners.

The hexagon has ___ sides and ___ corners.

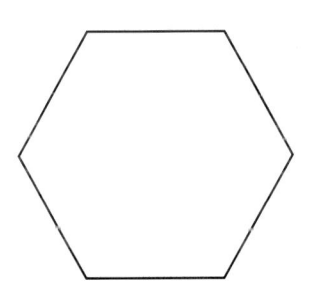

Shapes with a Rope © Rigby, 2004.
This page may be photocopied for educational use within the purchasing institution.

Stage B Book 4
Making Party Hats

Learning About	Three-element patterns
Strand	Number
Focus	Patterning with three repeating elements
Additional Concepts	Two-dimensional shapes, sequencing

Links with other PM Books
Red Block, Blue Block (Rigby PM Math Readers Stage A)
A Game with Shapes (Rigby PM Math Readers Stage A)
Big Shapes and Little Shapes (Rigby PM Math Readers Stage A)
Shapes with a Rope (Rigby PM Math Readers Stage B)

About the Book
A boy cuts out red, yellow, and blue circles, triangles, and squares. He glues these shapes in three-element repeating patterns, onto six strips of paper, to make party hats.

Mathematical language
six, triangle, square, circle, Saturday, long, first

High-frequency words
again, be, came, got, I'm, it, like, made, make, my, new, of, put, some, they, this, will, with, your
red, blue, yellow,

Focusing on the concept

- *Cover and title page:* Talk about the hats the six children are wearing. Notice that each one has a different pattern. Discuss how the hats could have been made.
- *Pages 2–5:* Discuss the preparation that Tim did prior to making the party hats.
- *Pages 6–9:* Read the text aloud with the children. Make sure they are aware of the way the color pattern is repeated.
- *Pages 10–13:* Encourage the children to make close connections between the photographs and the text.
- *Pages 14–16:* Reinforce the different patterns by "reading" each one aloud.

Reinforcing the concept

- Use everyday materials to make three-element repeated patterns, such as leaf, stick, stone; shoe, sandal, boot; knife, fork, spoon.
- Write high frequency words as repeating patterns, such as come, look, go; come, coming, came; look, book, cook.
- Discover repeated patterns of color on clothing, drapes, upholstery, etc.

Discovering additional concepts

- **Two-dimensional shapes:** Talk about the attributes of a triangle, a square, and a circle. List these attributes on a chart, such as *a triangle has three sides and three corners*.
- **Sequencing:** Have three children play a basic rhythm using a drum, castanets, and maracas. First individually and then together.

Using the blackline masters

1. Read the poem together. Talk about how to repeat the patterns and colors.
2. Make sure the children understand that they are to repeat the pattern and colors on each line. Children choose their colors, then color the shapes repeating the pattern and colors.
3. "Read" the patterns aloud. Establish the missing elements. Make sure the children understand how to make their own patterns using repeated shapes and colors.

Rigby PM Math Readers Teacher's Guide: Emergent

Name _____

Making Party Hat Patterns

I made a colored pattern on a party hat.
Red, blue, and yellow, the pattern goes like that.

red   blue   yellow   ____   ____   ____

yellow   red   blue   ____   ____   ____

Name _____

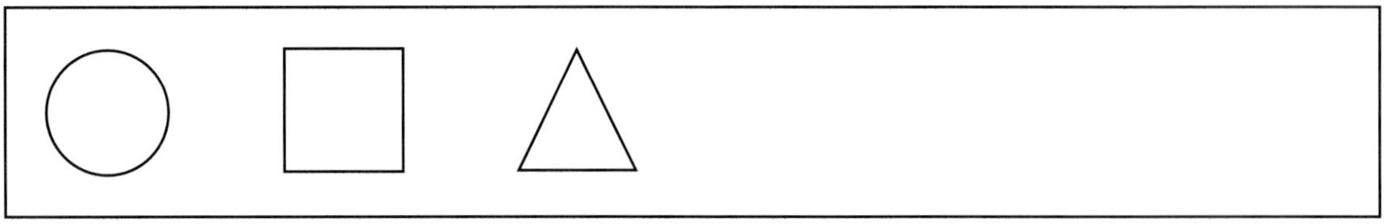

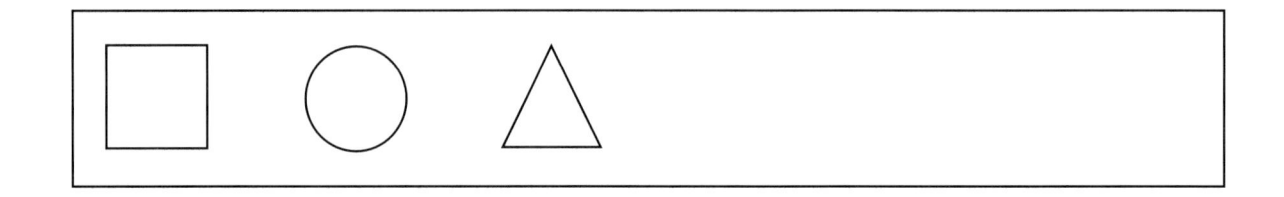

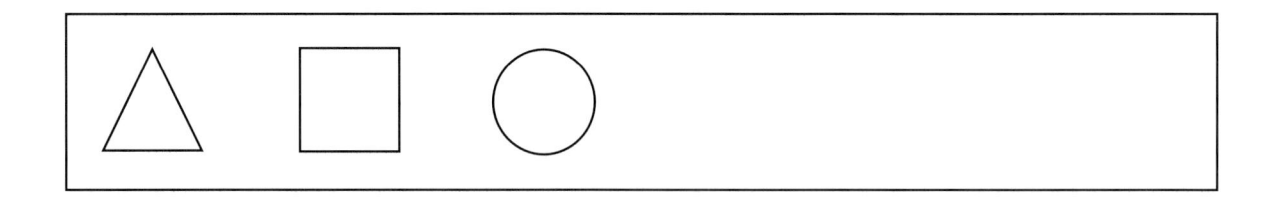

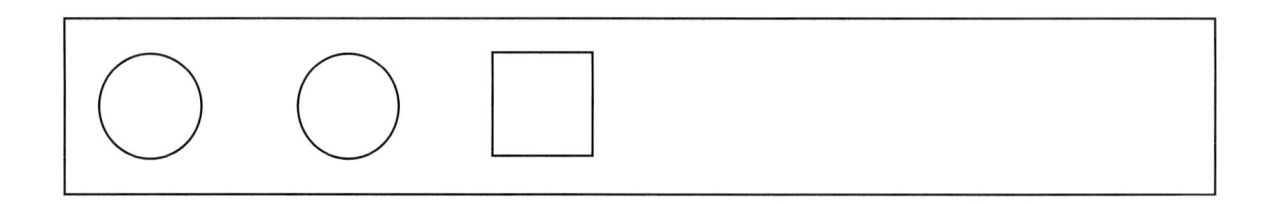

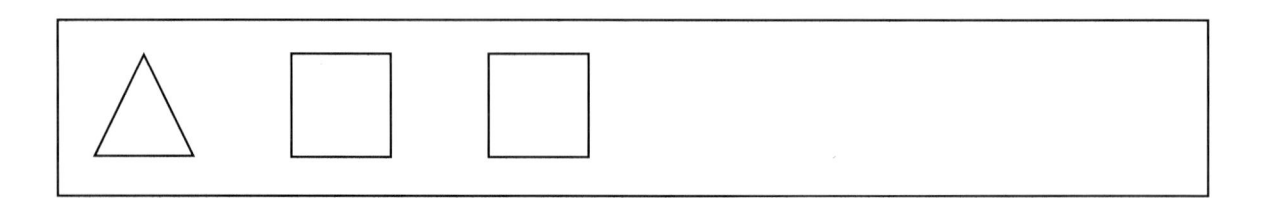

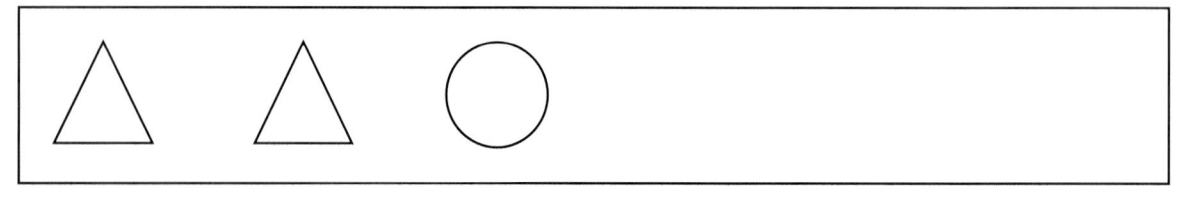

Rigby
PM Math Readers

78 *Making Party Hats* © Rigby, 2004.
This page may be photocopied for educational use within the purchasing institution.

Blackline master 2 *Rigby PM Math Readers Teacher's Guide: Emergent*

Name _____

Make your patterns with ○ □ △

Stage B Book 5
Boxes, Cans, and Balls

Learning About Three-dimensional shapes
Strand Shape and Space
Focus Identifying three-dimensional shapes by touch
Additional Concepts Properties of three-dimensional shapes, probability

Links with other PM Books
A Game with Shapes (Rigby PM Math Readers Stage A)
Shapes with a Rope (Rigby PM Math Readers Stage B)
Here come the shapes (PM Plus Level 6)

About the Book
Three children take turns to remove a box (cube), a can (cylinder) and a ball (sphere) from a bag using only the sense of touch.

Mathematical language
box, can, ball, first, inside, into, big, little

High-frequency words
again, all, back, find, her, his, it, like, play, put, they, this, where, with

Focusing on the concept

- *Cover and title page:* Read the title. Explain to the children the purpose of the game. Study each shape and discuss how to identify it by touch, such as *a can has no corners, it has a circle at each end, and it will roll.*
- *Pages 2–3:* Study each three-dimensional object from different angles. Ask: "What flat surfaces can you see?"
- *Pages 4–15:* Reinforce the procedures for playing the game, such as the children cannot look inside the bag and they must put the shape back in the bag before the next child has a turn. Ask questions like, "How did Sally know which was the little box?"
- *Page 16:* Review the properties of three-dimensional shapes, for example, sides, corners, edges; curved, round. Provide a variety of three-dimensional shapes that have similar properties for the children to sort and compare.

Reinforcing the concept

- Provide a bag and objects. Have three children demonstrate how to play the game. Encourage those watching to ask questions, such as "How did you know you had the little can?"
- Make three-dimensional shapes from clay.

Discovering additional concepts

- **Properties of three-dimensional shapes:** Find objects in the classroom that are shaped like a can, a box, or a ball. Sort the shapes into groups, such as *these shapes all have straight edges.*

  Take the children for a walk to observe shapes that have similar properties, for example, doors, windows, and tables.

- **Probability:** Put a blindfold on one child. Have another child hand the first child a box, ball, or can. Ask the blindfolded child to name the shape by touch.

Using the blackline masters

1. Read the verse and color the picture. Trace over the gray words and three-dimensional shapes.
2. Trace over the gray words and color the shapes to match the statements.
3. Trace over the gray words. Color the shapes to make the statements correct.

Name _____

Rigby PM Math Readers

Here is a bag

Filled with boxes, balls, and cans.

See what you can find

when you put in your hand.

boxes	
cans	
balls	

Boxes, Cans, and Balls © Rigby, 2004.
This page may be photocopied for educational use within the purchasing institution.

Blackline master 1 *Rigby PM Math Readers Teacher's Guide: Emergent*

Name _____

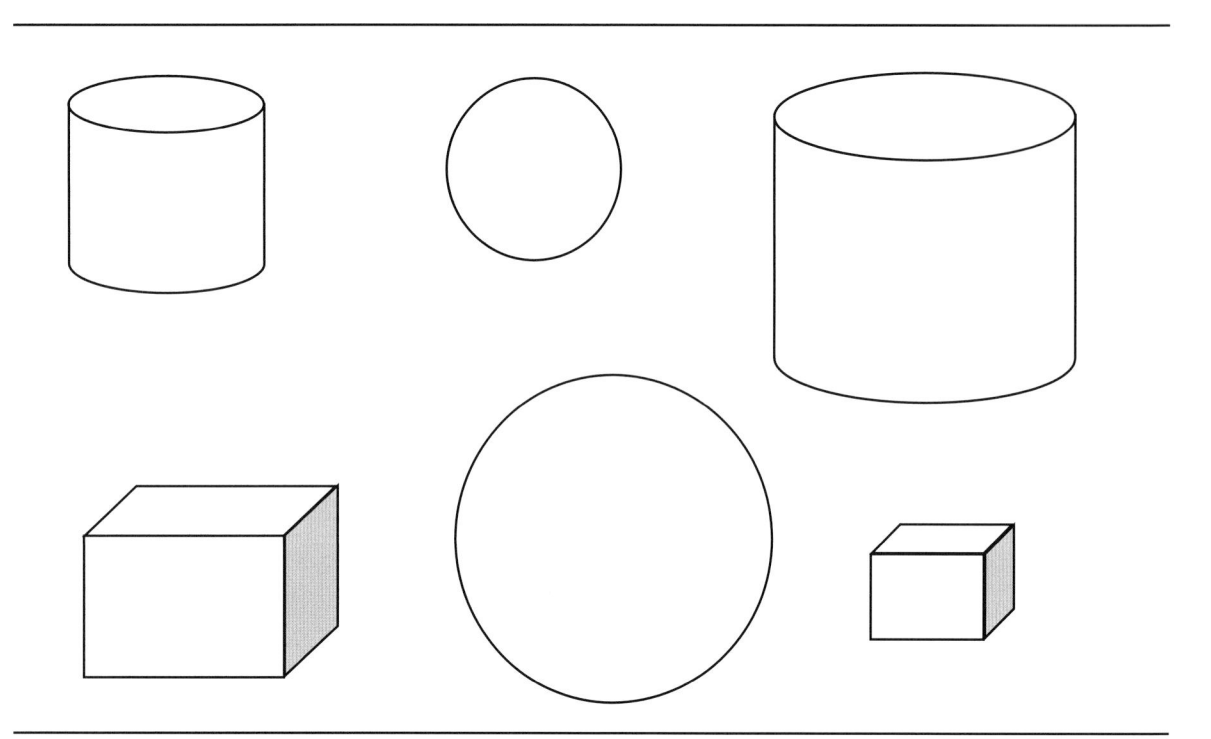

The little box is blue.

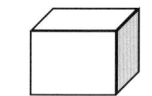

The big box is red.

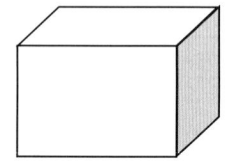

The little can is green.

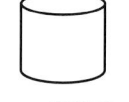

The big can is yellow.

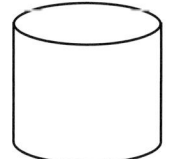

The little circle is red.

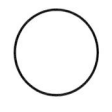

The big circle is blue.

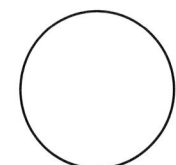

Name _____

All the boxes in the bag are green.

All the cans in the bag are red.

All the balls in the bag are blue.

Stage B Book 6
Six Under the Sea

Learning About	Six
Strand	Number
Focus	Groups of six in a range of patterns
Additional Concepts	Cardinal names and numbers, position and movement

Links with other PM Books
Four Cars (Rigby PM Math Readers Stage B)
Five Birds and Five Mice (Rigby PM Math Readers Stage B)
Animal Graphs (Rigby PM Math Readers Stage B)
Birthday balloons (PM Level 10)

About the Book
Six children make a mural showing groups of six things they would find under the sea. Each set reinforces different groupings or one-to-one correspondence.

Mathematical language	High-frequency words	Numeral
one, two, three, four, five, six, big, little, tiny, under, on, up, down,	after, by, children, made, of, put, they, went, will, red, blue, yellow, white, brown, green	6

Focusing on the concept

- *Cover and title page:* Read the title together. Make a list of things that could be under the sea. Discuss how to make a mural as a group activity.
- *Pages 2–3:* Observe that there is a group of six children making the mural. Discuss the grouping of the six little fish: 3, 2, and 1.
- *Pages 4–5:* Read aloud the text and predict how the six big fish will be grouped and where they will be placed on the mural.
- *Pages 6–9:* Talk about the line of rocks and red crabs reinforcing the concept of one-to-one correspondence.
- *Pages 10–13:* Discuss the new groupings. Record these as *3 and 3*, and as *2, 2, and 2*.
- *Pages 14–16:* Talk about the completed mural, again drawing the children's attention to the groupings, colors, and size relationships.

Reinforcing the concept

- Have a group of six children make a mural about six things they would see *At the Zoo*, *In the Garden* or *On the Beach*. Encourage the children to discuss the groupings of each set.
- Show the children how to fold a sheet of paper into six equal pieces. Draw an insect in each piece, such as a ladybug or a bee. Explain that insects have six legs. Draw the six legs on each insect.

Discovering additional concepts

- **Cardinal names and numbers:** Discuss where the number **six** comes in relation to the numbers **one** to **ten**. Use a number line to reinforce the understanding of **before, after,** and **between.**
- **Position and movement:** Review positional language that has been used in the text: **under, after, on, up,** and **down.**

Using the blackline masters

1. Read the poem together. Talk about an appropriate illustration. Color the fish in the illustration at the bottom of the page and complete the missing numerals.
2. Find each set of six in the book. Encourage the children to draw sets with different groupings.
3. Make sure the children understand how to plan their two sets of drawings.

Name _____

Rigby **PM Math Readers**

Six Under the Sea

Six little gray fish

swimming in the sea,

here come six big fish

as hungry as can be.

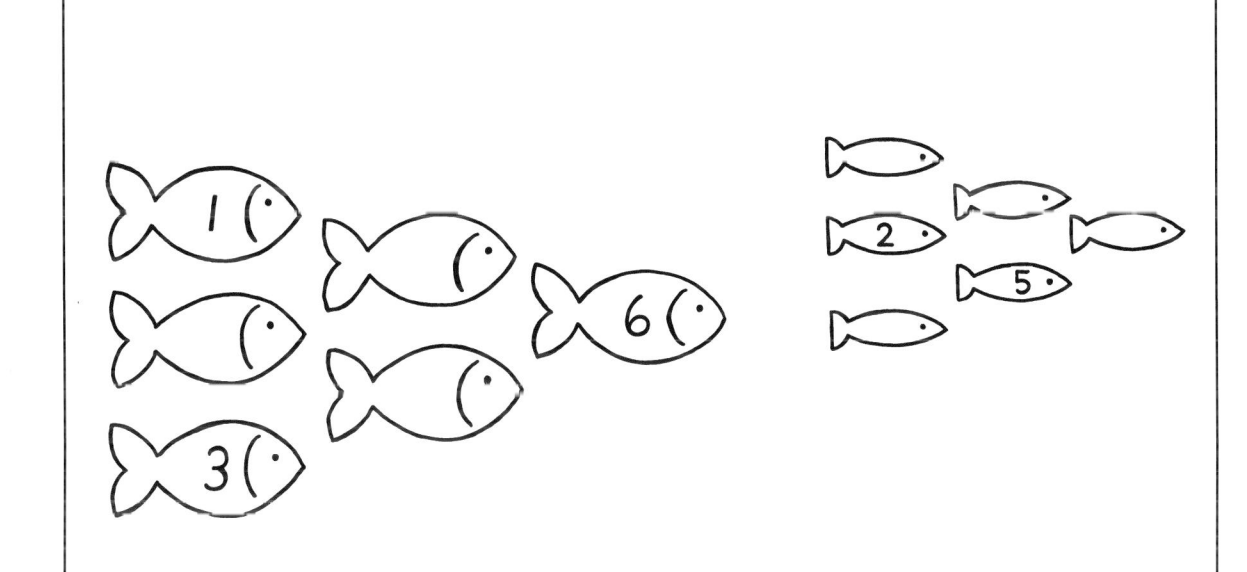

Six big fish and _____ little fish.

Six Under the Sea © Rigby, 2004.
This page may be photocopied for educational use within the purchasing institution.

Blackline master 1 Rigby PM Math Readers Teacher's Guide: Emergent   85

Name _____

Six Under the Sea

6 big fish	6 little fish
6 brown rocks	6 red crabs
6 white shells	6 tiny sea horses

Name _____

Six Up in the Sky

Draw 6 bees and 6 butterflies up in the sky.

Stage B Book 7
Seven in a Line

Learning About	Seven
Strand	Number
Focus	Sequencing seven objects according to size
Additional Concepts	Three-dimensional shapes, ordinal names

Links with other PM Books
My tower (PM Plus Level 4)
The go-karts (PM Starters 1)
Balloons (PM Plus Level 1)

About the Book
Seven children put sets of seven three-dimensional shapes, and themselves, in order of size. The first two sets are in vertical order; the other two are in horizontal order.

Mathematical language	High-frequency words	Numeral
one, two, three, four, five, six, seven, big, biggest, small, smallest, first, last, box, can, ball, top, line	all, but, can't, children, have, made, of, some, who, will, with	7

Focusing on the concept

- *Cover and title page:* Discuss the concept of measurement by height (the children on the cover) and size (the balls on the title page), and the sequential forming of the lines.
- *Pages 2–3:* Using the title page as a guide, ask the children to predict the order that they think the boxes will go in – focus on the smallest box and the largest box.
- *Pages 4–5:* Confirm that the linear order of the boxes suggested by the children is the same order as shown in the tower.
- *Pages 6–9:* Reinforce the concepts that have been discussed on the previous pages.
- *Pages 10–16:* Discuss the reasons why the balls cannot be placed in vertical order. Focus on the fact that the balls are graded in linear order according to size (mass) and the children are graded according to size (height).

Reinforcing the concept

- Measure the heights of a group of children and put them in sequential order. Reverse the line in descending order. Discuss similarities.
- Find objects to form sequential lines and towers. Put the lines in descending order, and discuss problems associated with inverting the towers.

Discovering additional concepts

- **Three-dimensional shapes:** Compare the properties of the cube, sphere, and cylinder. Use terms such as **sides, corners, faces, flat surfaces,** and **curved surfaces.**
- **Ordinal names:** Focus on the terms **first** and **last** (as they relate to the lines and towers). Introduce ordinal names from **second** to **seventh.** Children in sequential order can say, for example, "I am first in the line."

Using the blackline masters

1. Read the verse and color the picture. Count and color the cans. Trace and complete the gray numerals and words. Complete and color the circles, and write the correct numeral under each one.
2. Trace the words. Complete the lines of shapes according to size, and then color them.
3. Color and cut out the shapes. Glue onto cardboard in order.

Name _____

Rigby
PM Math
Readers

Seven in a Line

All our friends are standing here.

Seven children in a line.

Some are big and some are small.

I am short and you are tall.

seven cans	
7	7 _ _ _ _ _ _ _
seven	seven _ _ _ _ _ _
seven circles	○ ○ ○

Seven in a Line © Rigby, 2004.
This page may be photocopied for educational use within the purchasing institution.

Blackline master 1 *Rigby PM Math Readers Teacher's Guide: Emergent* 89

Name _____

Rigby PM Math Readers

Seven circles in a line.

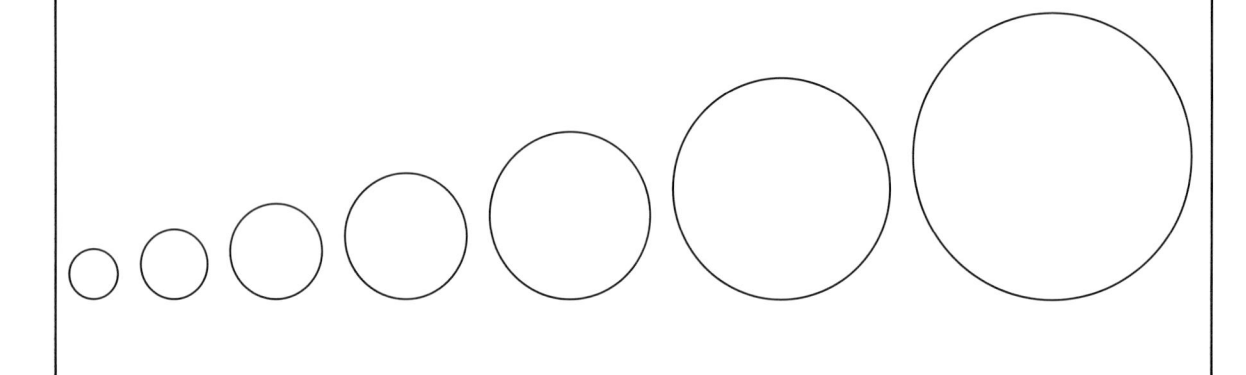

Seven triangles in a line.

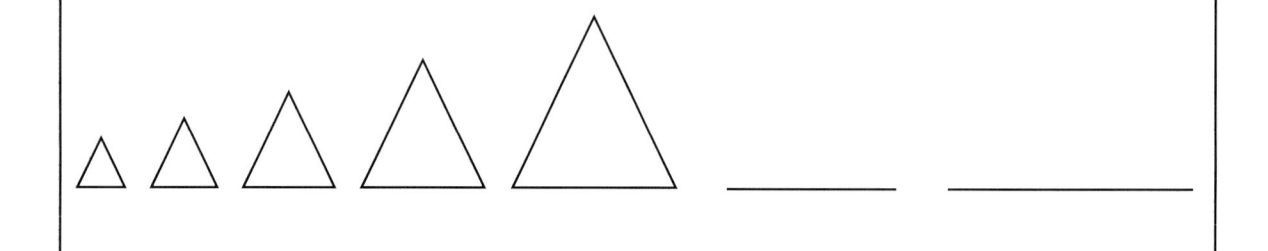

Seven rectangles in a line.

90 *Seven in a Line* © Rigby, 2004.
This page may be photocopied for educational use within the purchasing institution.

Blackline master 2 *Rigby PM Math Readers Teacher's Guide: Emergent*

Name _____

Stage B Book 8
From One to Eight

Learning About	Eight
Strand	Number
Focus	Numerical order
Additional Concepts	Position and direction, ordinal names

Links with other PM Books
My tower (PM Plus Level 4)
Seven in a Line (Rigby PM Math Readers Stage B)
The Class Photo (Rigby PM Math Readers Stage D)

About the Book
Following instructions, two children place numeral cards in sequential horizontal order from one to eight.

Mathematical language	High-frequency words	Numerals
one, eight, line, numbers, count, first, second, third, last	after, again, all, but, by, can't, from, get, it, make, now, teacher, this, will, with	1, 2, 3, 4, 5, 6, 7, 8

Focusing on the concept

- *Cover and title page:* Ask the children to look at the disordered numbers on the table in the cover picture, and point to them in order as they count to eight. Then turn to the title page and check the correct positional order.
- *Pages 2–3:* The children can read the directions and predict, or point to, the number card that will go first in the line.
- *Pages 4–15:* As the children read each page, they can make predictions as to which number will be next in line. They can then check the picture on the following page to see if they were correct.
- *Page 16:* Count the numbers forward and backward with the children. Comment on the fact that the position and order of the numbers remains constant.

Reinforcing the concept

- Count the line of seals on the blackboard. Make connections with the seals and the numerals, comparing the position of each seal with its corresponding number.

Discovering additional concepts

- **Position and direction:** Discuss the fact that the line of numbers starts on the left and moves to the right, and that this is the same direction in which the words in the text are read. Use positional vocabulary to describe the order that the numbers are in, such as **comes after, comes before, is next to,** and **is beside.**
- **Ordinal names:** Focus on the words **first, second, third,** and **last.** Use the completed line of numerals, and the seals, to introduce ordinal names for the remaining positions.

Using the blackline masters

1. Read the verse and color the picture. Complete the numerals on the "cards." Trace and complete the gray numerals and words. Complete and color the circles, and write the correct numeral under each one.
2. Trace over the gray words and numerals. Complete the missing numerals in the spaces.
3. Trace over the numerals. Cut out the numeral cards and put them in the correct order from 1 to 8. Then put them in reverse order. Say the number names.

Name _____

From One to Eight

1, 2, 3, 4, 5, 6, 7,

Here is 8… our line is done.

You can count from 1 to 8,

I will count from 8 to 1.

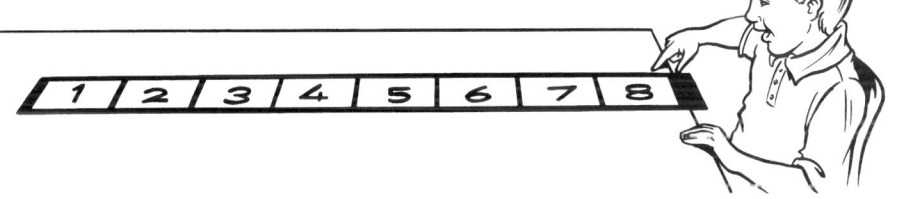

1 to 8	1	2	3					
8	8 __ __ __ __ __ __ __								
eight	eight __ __ __ __ __ __ __								
eight circles	○ ○ ○ ○								

Name _____

From one to eight

1   2   3   4   5   6   7   8

From one **to** eight

1   __   __   4   __   __   __   8

From eight to one

8   7   6   5   4   3   2   1

From eight **to** one

8   __   __   __   4   __   __   1

Name _____

Rigby PM Math Readers

1
8
7
4
6
2
5
3

From One to Eight © Rigby, 2004.
This page may be photocopied for educational use within the purchasing institution.

Blackline master 3 *Rigby PM Math Readers Teacher's Guide: Emergent*

Stage B Book 9

Nine Children at the Pool

Learning About	Nine
Strand	Number
Focus	Compensation of a number
Additional Concepts	Addends of nine, ordered and disordered groups

Links with other PM Books
The farmer in the dell (PM Readalongs)
The Four Cars (Rigby PM Math Readers Stage A)
Five Birds and Five Mice (Rigby PM Math Readers Stage A)

About the Book
This illustrated story shows nine children entering a swimming pool one by one. The series of related equations shows ways of forming nine as a sum of two addends.

Mathematical language	High-frequency words	Numerals
one, two, three, four, five, six, seven, eight, nine, line	all, boy, children, have, having, they	1, 2, 3, 4, 5, 6, 7, 8, 9

Focusing on the concept

- *Cover and title page:* Count the children on the cover, and again on the title page. Confirm that children remain in their same positions in the line as they move towards the ladder.
- *Pages 2–3:* Count the children again. Connect the numerals on page 2 with the corresponding children on page 3. Predict which child might enter the pool first. Discuss the number of children waiting, and compare with the number in the pool. Introduce the term **zero**.
- *Pages 4–15:* Read aloud the text and make equations orally, based on the text. Record equations on a chart. Count the children in the pool and outside the pool to confirm. Predict which child will enter the pool next, and locate the children on each page.
- *Page 16:* Read the equations, and connect with the colored circles. Check against those recorded on the chart. Confirm that they are identical.

Reinforcing the concept

- Use counters to show compensation of a range of numbers below ten. Make labels with written equations to place beside the counters.
- Play "The farmer in the dell" with up to a total of nine children in the circle.

Discovering additional concepts

- **Addends of nine:** Observe that two situations ("out of the pool" and "in the pool") are required to form two addends. Note that the total remains constant as the addends change.
- **Ordered and disordered groups:** Observe the two sets of groupings shown in each picture. Discuss the reasons why it is easier to recognize a total number of units when they are placed in order, such as in a line or a pattern, compared with a disordered group.

Using the blackline masters

1. Read the verse and color the picture. Count and color the children in line. Trace and complete the gray numerals and words. Complete and color the circles and write the correct numeral under each one.

2. Trace over the gray words. Draw nine children in the pool and color the picture.

3. Trace over the gray words and numerals. Write the missing numerals in the spaces.

Name _____

Rigby PM Math Readers

Nine Children at the Pool

Nine little children came from school. They are swimming in the pool.

nine children	
9	9 _ _ _ _ _ _ _ _
nine	nine _ _ _ _ _ _
nine circles	○ ○ ○ ○ ○

Nine Children at the Pool © Rigby, 2004.
This page may be photocopied for educational use within the purchasing institution.

Blackline master 1 *Rigby PM Math Readers Teacher's Guide: Emergent*

Name _____

Nine children are in the pool.

One, two, three, four, five, six, seven, eight, nine.

Name _____

Rigby PM Math Readers

zero + nine = nine	0 and 9
one + eight = nine	1 and 8
two + seven = nine	2 and __
three + six = nine	3 and __
four + five = nine	4 and __
five + four = _____	5 and __
six + three = _____	6 and __
seven + two = _____	7 and __
eight + one = _____	__ and __

Nine Children at the Pool © Rigby, 2004.
This page may be photocopied for educational use within the purchasing institution.

Blackline master 3 *Rigby PM Math Readers Teacher's Guide: Emergent*

Stage B Book 10
Five and Five are Ten

Learning About Ten
Strand Number
Focus Conservation of a number
Additional Concepts Counting, addition

Links with other PM Books
Five Birds and Five Mice (Rigby PM Math Readers Stage A)
Sally's beans (PM Level 6)
Ten Frogs for the Pond (Rigby PM Math Readers Stage B)

About the Book
A text in verse, based on a variety of addends which have a sum of ten. Each set of two addends becomes three addends on the following page.

Mathematical language	High-frequency words	Numerals
one, two, three, four, five, six, seven, eight, nine, ten, add	again, all, but, if, that, will	1, 2, 3, 4, 5, 6, 7, 8, 9, 10

Focusing on the concept

- *Cover and title page:* Connect the title on the cover with the patterns of five, and with the statement on the chalkboard. Observe the various ways of representing the number ten on the title page.
- *Pages 2–5:* Introduce the rhythm of the verse, and the way it describes the equations. Discuss the similarities and differences in the equations. Connect the words in the text with the number patterns and numerals. Establish recognition of the number patterns. Note that the first addend remains constant.
- *Pages 6–15:* Children can predict possible numbers that could be used for the three-addend equations. (Note that all addends are valid, not just those used in the book.)
- *Page 16:* Discuss the recorded equations, and add to them.

Reinforcing the concept

- Use magnetic counters to form a variety of three-addend equations that have a sum of ten. Base further verses on these equations.
- Change the order of the two-addend equations, and the relevant words in the verse. Use more than three addends.

Discovering additional concepts

- **Counting:** Use counting as a method of checking the totals in the number patterns. Count the number of addends in each equation and relate to the equivalent numeral.
- **Addition:** Reinforce the use of **and** as the word which represents addition, and **are** which defines the sum. This book can also be used with the equation symbols + and =.

Using the blackline masters

1. Read the verse and color the picture. Trace over the statement, and write the correct numerals under the words. Trace and complete the gray numerals and words. Complete and color the circles, and write the correct numeral under each one.
2. Trace over the gray words and numerals. Add the correct number pattern to the blank cards.
3. Trace over the gray numerals. Add numerals in the spaces. Add the correct number patterns to the blank cards.

Rigby PM Math Readers Teacher's Guide: Emergent

Name _____

Five and Five are Ten

Five and five are ten,

and if we look again,

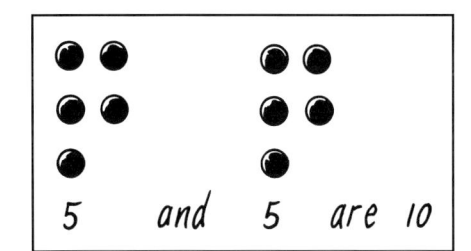

5 and 5 are 10

we see that five and three and two

will all add up to ten.

5 and 3 and 2 are 10

5 and 5 are 10	five and five are ten
10	10 ___ ___ ___ ___
ten	ten ___ ___ ___ ___
ten circles	○ ○ ○

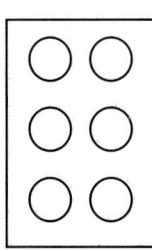

Name _____

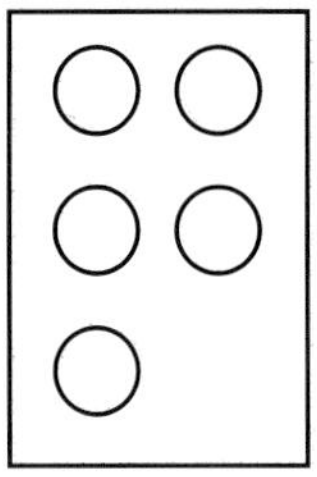

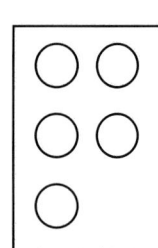

five + five = ten

six + four = ten

7 + 3 = 10

8 + 2 = 10

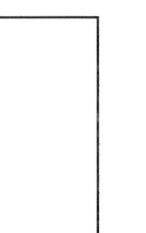

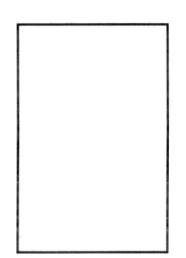

Name _____

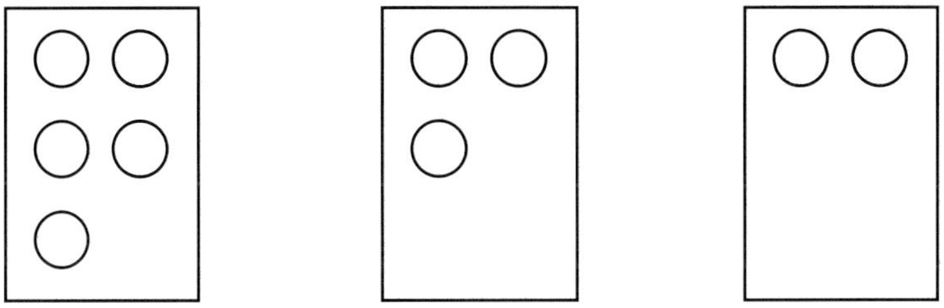

5 + 3 + 2 = 10

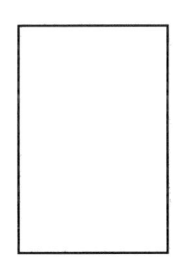

4 + 3 + 3 = ___

3 + 4 + ___ = 10

2 + 4 + ___ = 10

Stage B Book 11
Ten Frogs for the Pond

Learning About Strand	Chance
Focus	Number
	Probability and chance
Additional Concepts	Addition, the empty set, zero

Links with other PM Books
Five and Five are Ten (Rigby PM Math Readers Stage B)
Animal Graphs (Rigby PM Math Readers Stage B)
Grouping Shells (Rigby PM Math Readers Stage C)

About the Book
Two children play a board game involving chance and grouping addends to ten.

Mathematical language	High-frequency words
one, two, three, four, five, ten, first, under	do, find, has, have, I'm, make, they, this green, yellow, red, orange,

Focusing on the concept

- *Cover and title page:* Talk about the title and connect it to the picture on the board game. Discuss the four boxes and the ten frog counters in relation to the game.
- *Pages 2–3:* Read and discuss the text. Make sure the children understand the rules of the game.
- *Pages 4–9:* Write the number story on a chalkboard. Discuss the empty set.
- *Pages 10–15:* After reading these pages write this new number story under the first one. Then have the children demonstrate how the process involves chance.
- *Page 16:* Count the frogs in each set and relate them to the numerals in the number sentence. Make sure the children understand the relationship between the numeral **0,** the word **zero,** and the concept of **the empty set.**

Reinforcing the concept

- Play similar games of chance:
  Hide ten small objects, such as toy cars, in groups behind/inside/under specific items. There may be two, three or four specific items to practice the grouping concept.
  Toss five small beanbags into a circle. Increase the distance between the circle and the point of throwing at each new attempt.

Discovering additional concepts

- **Addition:** Make up a similar playing board. This time use a different theme, such as monkeys in a tree. Use counters. Encourage the children to discover other groupings. Write and illustrate these groupings. Talk about **adding on.**
- **The empty set:** Make a chart showing the addition of **zero,** such as 1 and 0, and 2 and 0.

Using the blackline masters

1. Read the poem together. Explain that the four boxes are to be colored then groups of frogs drawn below three of them.
2. Show the children how to use counters to find the answers.
3. Explain how to count the frogs then fill in the missing numerals.

Name _____

Ten Frogs for the Pond

Ten frogs are hiding,

where they can't be seen.

Are they under the orange box…

or yellow… or red… or green?

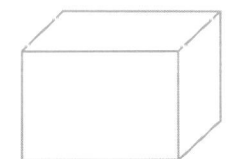

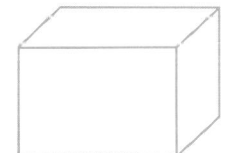

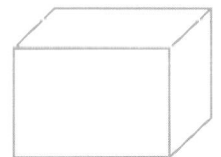

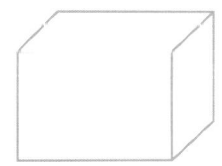

Name _____

Two and three make ☐

Four and five make ☐

One and seven and two make ☐

Five and three and two make ☐

Name _____

5 and 4 and ___ make 10

6 and 3 and ___ make 10

7 and 2 and ___ make 10

8 and 1 and ___ make 10

9 and 0 and ___ make 10

Ten Frogs for the Pond © Rigby, 2004.
This page may be photocopied for educational use within the purchasing institution.

Stage B Book 12
Animal Graphs

Learning About Graphs
Strand Data
Focus Grouping and comparing
Additional Concepts Analyzing data, part/whole relationships

Links with other PM Books
Ten Frogs for the Pond (Rigby PM Math Readers Stage B)
Look at the Leaves (Rigby PM Math Readers Stage A)
Five and Five are Ten (Rigby PM Math Readers Stage B)

About the Book
A group of ten children make two picture-graphs about animals. They arrange the pictures on a circular graph shape before discussing and analyzing the information.

Mathematical language
one, two, three, five, six, graph, Monday, Tuesday

High-frequency words
children, help, it, like, made, make, of, put, some, teacher, they, this, today, with

Focusing on the concept

- *Cover and title page:* Read the title. Talk about the pictures the children have cut out and the way they have been arranged in a circular form to make a graph.
- *Pages 2–3:* Notice that the children still have more animals to put on the graph.
- *Pages 4–5:* Discuss Kim's statement.
- *Pages 6–15:* Encourage the children to use comparative phrases, such as **more than,** and **fewer than,** as they discuss the pictures on page 8. Count all of the animals on page 13. Discuss Daniel's statement on page 14.
- *Page 16:* Compare the information on the two graphs.

Reinforcing the concept

- Arrange a set of five plastic blocks in an line. Arrange another set of plastic blocks in a disordered group. Compare the two groups. Does one set have more than the other? Why?
- Encourage the children to identify groups within groups. Teach the skill of counting on from the larger group.

Discovering additional concepts

- **Analyzing data:** Re-read *Look at the Leaves* (Rigby PM Math Readers Stage A). Teach the skill of analyzing information using comparative words and phrases, such as **most, more than,** and **fewer than.**
- **Part/whole relationships:** Paste a picture of an animal or a vehicle onto cardboard. Cut the picture into three different size pieces. Reassemble to make the picture.

Using the blackline masters

1. Read the poem together. Discuss how to complete the shapes graph.
2. Count the pictures of the cats, birds, and dogs. Explain how to cut around each dotted circle and how to place each one in the appropriate space on the graph. Complete the labels.
3. Make sure the children know how to complete each section. Compare the information in the ordered and disordered groups.

Name _____

Rigby PM Math Readers

Animal Graphs

We made a graph with animals,

for all of you to see.

Which is the one we like the best,

six or one or three?

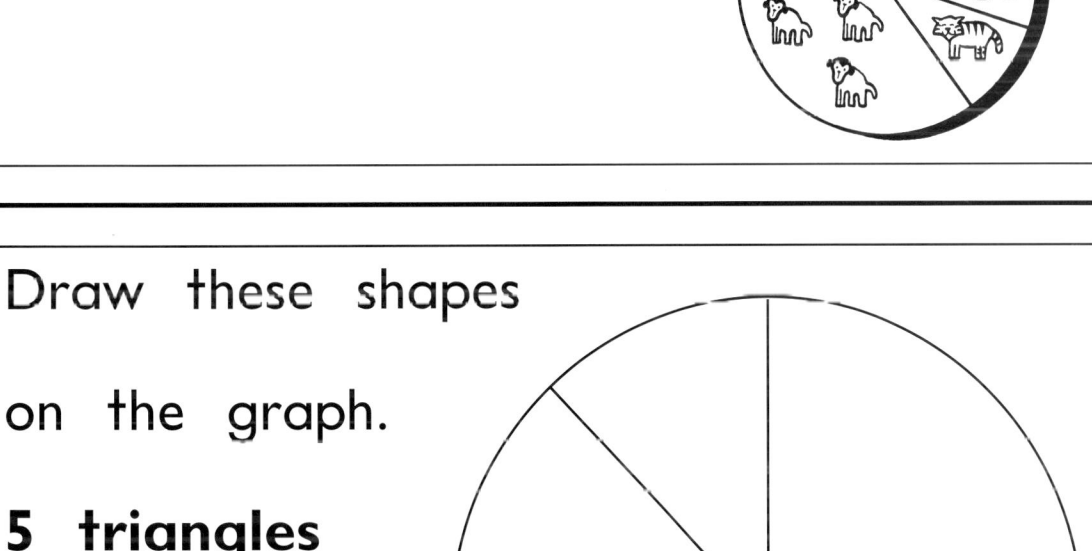

Draw these shapes on the graph.

5 triangles

4 squares

1 circle

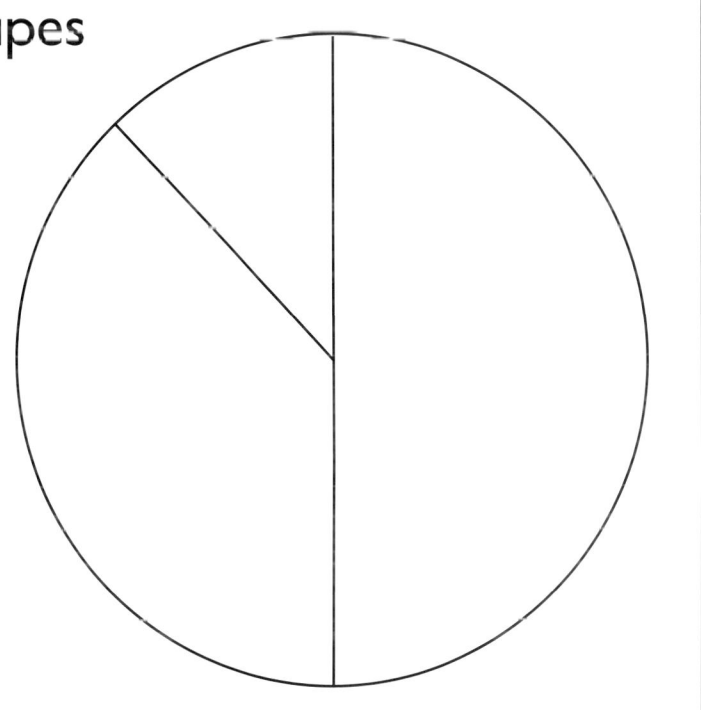

Animal Graphs © Rigby, 2004.
This page may be photocopied for educational use within the purchasing institution.

Blackline master 1 *Rigby PM Math Readers Teacher's Guide: Emergent* 109

Name _____

Rigby PM Math Readers

Pets Graph

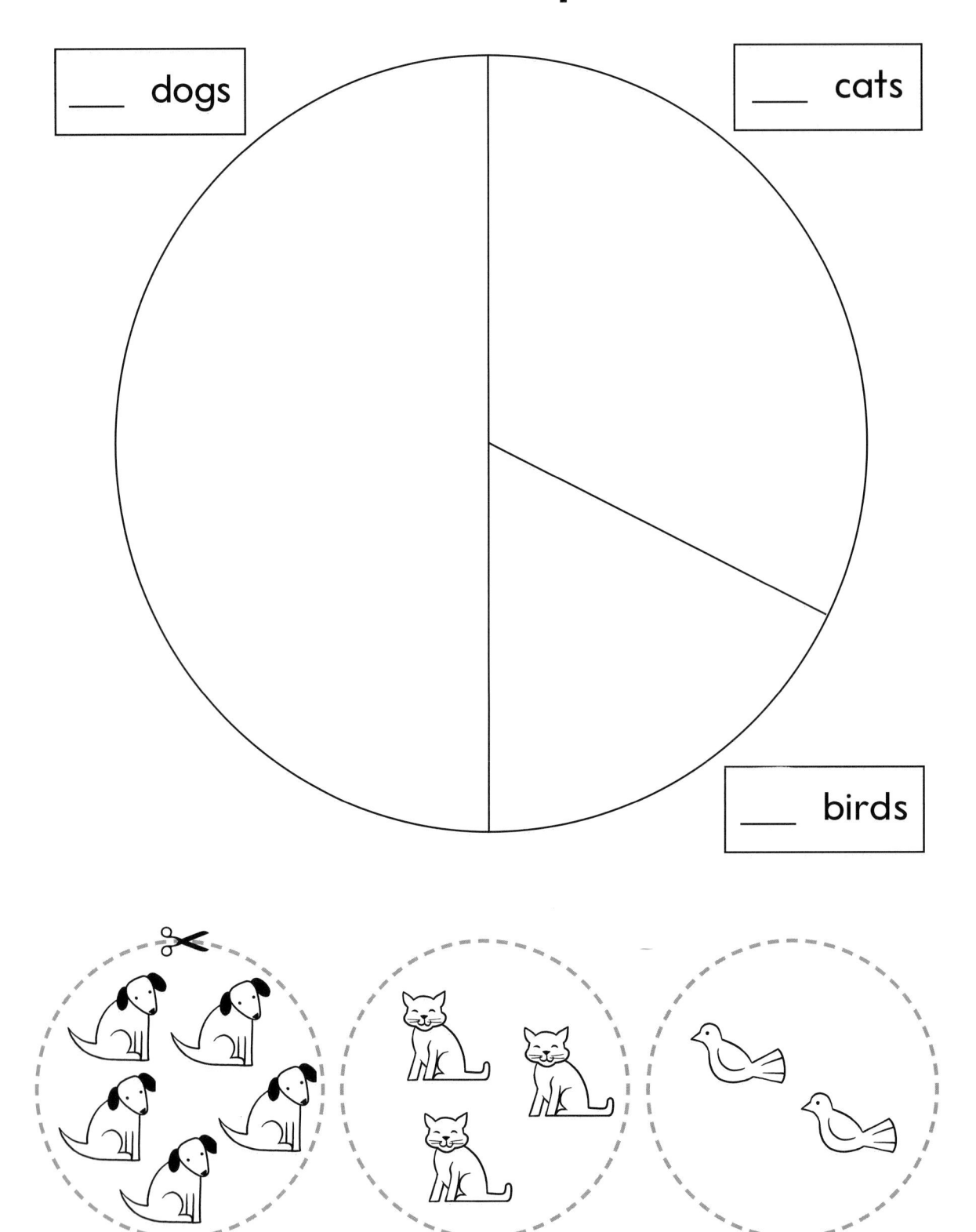

___ dogs

___ cats

___ birds

---

110 *Animal Graphs* © Rigby, 2004.
This page may be photocopied for educational use within the purchasing institution.

Blackline master 2 *Rigby PM Math Readers Teacher's Guide: Emergent*

Name _____

Favorite Fruit Graph

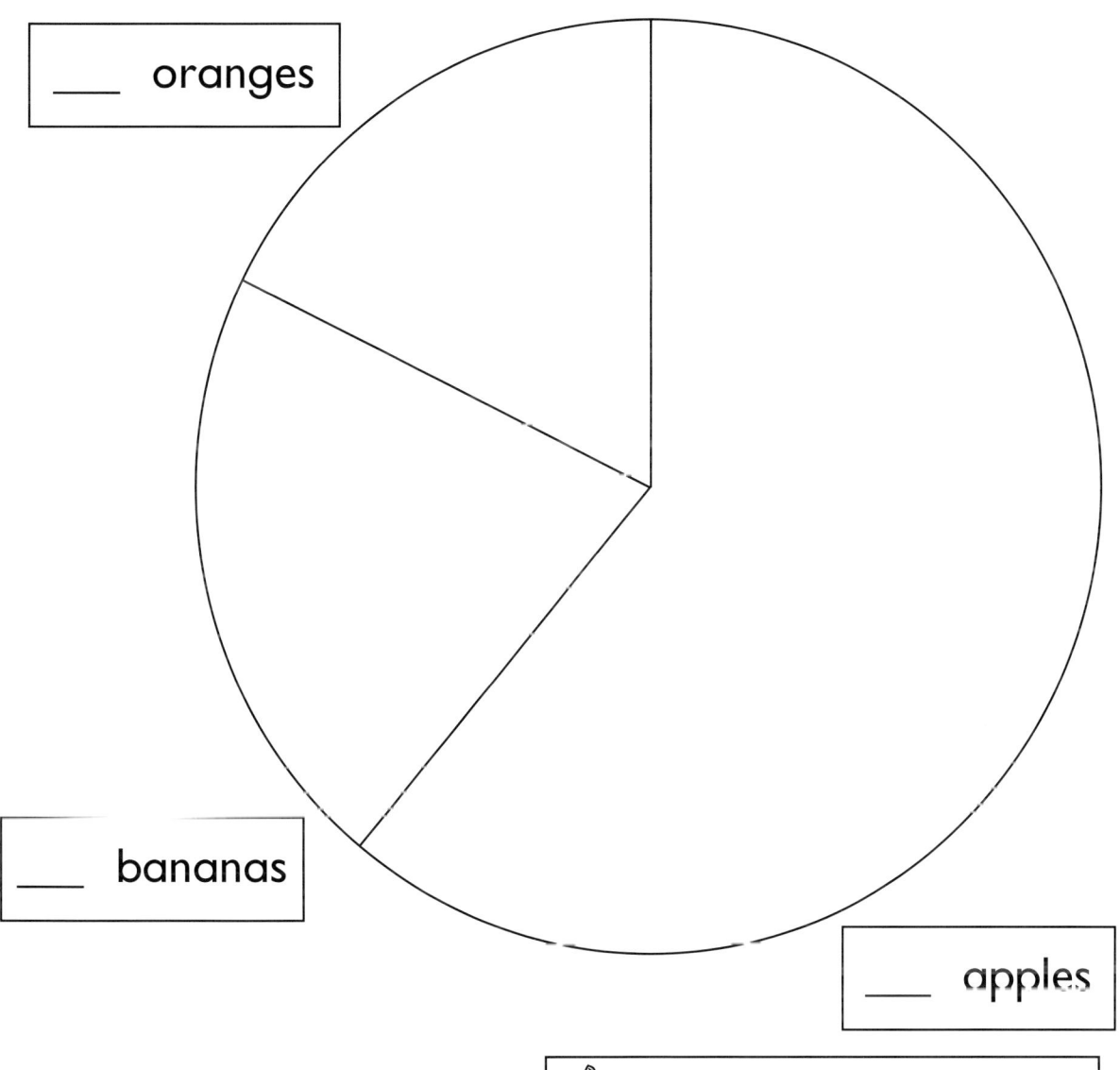

___ oranges

___ bananas

___ apples

Six children like apples.

Two children like bananas.

Two children like oranges.

Rigby PM Math Readers Concepts and Reading Levels

Building of High-frequency Words → **Gentle Gradient of Word Introduction**

Reading Levels

PM Reading Levels	Magenta Levels 1–2	Red Levels 3–5	Yellow Levels 6–8	Blue Levels 9–11	Green Levels 12–14	Orange Levels 15–16	Turquoise Levels 17–18
Stages of PM Math Readers	Stage A	Stage B		Stage C		Stage D	
Grade Level	Kindergarten			Grade 1			

112 Rigby PM Math Readers Teacher's Guide: Emergent